WOMEN, INK.
777 UNITED NATIONS PLAZA
NEW YORK, N.Y. 10017

WOMEN WORKING TOGETHER

for personal, economic, and community development

A handbook of activities for
women's learning and action groups

by Suzanne Kindervatter

OEF INTERNATIONAL
"Since 1947, helping women to help themselves."

About the Author

Suzanne Kindervatter, ED.D., is OEF's Director of Technical Services, a specialist in non-formal education, and a noted author and editor of training materials including the OEF series "Appropriate Business Skills for Third World Women."

Production Manager: Nena Terrell
Original Design: Paddy McLaughlin
Editorial Assistant: Anna Corrales
Artwork from Thailand: Athorn Kamasiri
Photos: Patti Burke
　　　　　Suzanne Kindervatter
　　　　　Deborah Ziska
　　　　　Scott Lewis

Distributed by:

WOMEN, INK.
777 United Nations Plaza
New York, N.Y. 10017 USA
Tel: (212) 687 - 8633
Fax: (212) 661 - 2704

© 1991 UNIFEM, all rights reserved

©1987 OEF International
ISBN #0 - 912917 - 03 - 2

Spanish edition printed in 1993 as
Las Mujeres Trabajan Unidas
French edition printed in 1987 as
Femmes, travaillons ensemble!
ISBN #0 - 912917 - 18 - 0
Library of Congress Card Catalogue #87 - 31276

Dedication

This handbook grew out of the experiences and contributions of many people. It is dedicated to the memory of two women whose effective personal lives were consistent with its purpose and whose talents were frequently devoted to helping and encouraging others:

Meredith Slobod Crist
and
Mary Cockefair Holt

Introduction

OEF International is proud to share with you *Women Working Together for Personal, Economic and Community Development.*

In its 40 years of experience providing technical assistance to women's groups worldwide, OEF has become acutely aware of the growing demand for training methodologies that address the particular needs of low-income women. The learning activities of this handbook—rooted in OEF training programs in Asia, Latin America, the Middle East and Africa—enable women to learn to work together more effectively to gain the confidence necessary to improve their lives and to take collective action to institute these economic and social changes.

Women Working Together is a vitally important contribution to the field of "women in development." It is a foundation upon which can be built a global network of women who, through increased self-reliance, will join together to improve the lives of their families and their communities.

I wish to thank all those who worked so hard to develop *Women Working Together,* especially the author, Dr. Suzanne Kindervatter, whose expertise in nonformal education and in the implementation of economic development training programs for women has led to the creation of this invaluable tool.

Elise Fiber Smith

Elise Fiber Smith
Executive Director
OEF International
1983

With thanks to many

Women working together in several countries around the world gave life to this handbook. The handbook testifies to the creativity and power of women who link their abilities and spirits.

I offer sincere appreciation and admiration to these women and to others who contributed to the handbook's development.

The "Human Development Project" of the *Federación de Organizaciones Voluntarias* in Costa Rica evolved a human development training approach that inspired this handbook. Gilma Palacios served as Project Director and Yiya Ortuño as Training Director.

The Federación de Asociaciones Femeninas Hondureñas (FAFH) in Honduras and the Northeast *Regional Training Center (NERTC) (Division of Land Settlements, Ministry of Interior, Government of Thailand)* in Thailand sponsored projects that used and refined the "Women Working Together" handbook. Special thanks to the following staff members of these organizations for their faith and commitment.

In Honduras: Dr. Norma Marina Garcia, President of FAFH; Dr. Alba de Quesada, Coordinator of the Legal Services Project; Ana Reyes de Baide, Coordinator for North Coast Puerto Cortés; Elia Luz de Alberty, Coordinator for San Pedro Sula; and Coordinators Martha de Jesús Diaz, Horten-Fonseca Espinal, Edith Falck, Doris G. Hernandez, Violeta Martinez, and Mercedes Rios.

In Thailand: Project Coordinators Siriporn Chamaporn, Buppa Meesaophet, and Nipaporn Harchai; Susan Saengprueng, NERTC Director; Athorn Shamasiri, NERTC Artist; Kanitha Chareonpool, Coordinator, Land Settlements Division, Bangkok; and Somvong Vongvornsang, Deputy Director, Land Settlements Division, Bangkok. Thanks also for the support of the Lam Phaow Land Settlement Superintendent Soonton Surinta and the Nai Amphur of Sahassakhan.

The village learning group leaders in Thailand and the group facilitators in Honduras gave so much of themselves in organizing and activating women in their communities. This handbook truly would not have been possible without their dedication.

In Thailand: Si Boonsai; Somwong Chai Kammi; Boonhom Hawnsombat; Tongsai Kanankang; Boonmaa Kulnthep; Basan Phimthasawn; Panomlak Phooalum, Chawee Phootthaisong; Maa Priw-asana; Kamwaan Saisi; Ratti Sangjan; Khak Sikammun; Witnam Sikawachai; Somwong Tammarak; Banchon Tipiyasen; Duangjai Wanyam; Champi Witchiensan; and Tan Yansawang.

In Honduras: Olga de Argueta; Maria Teresa de Castro; Romelia Gonzalez de Gallo; Graciela de Herrera; Eda Ramos de Hughes-Hallett; Carmen Isabel Poublanc de Melendez; Yolanda de Raudales; Herenia Marquez Soto; Gregoria B. de Varela; Guadalupe Valladares Velasquez; and Hilda Coello Zavala.

The projects in Thailand and Honduras were provided financial support by the U.S. Agency for International Development. Appreciation in particular goes to Bob Traister and Lawan Ratanaruang, U.S. AID Thailand, and to Roma Knee, AID Washington.

Financial support for the handbook production was generously provided through Jeanne Slobod, OEF Trustee; Charles Holt, OEF friend and former Board Member, and the ARCO Foundation.

Margaret Schuler, Technical Advisor for the OEF Central America Legal Services Project, provided invaluable assistance for the handbook program in Honduras and keen analysis of ways to strengthen the handbook. Sally Rudney, OEF Program Associate and handbook production manager, shared in the joys and challenges of completing the handbook. Her support, her utter competence, and her friendship were essential in getting the handbook done. Susan Roche, OEF Director for Women in Development Technical Advisory Services, gave excellent suggestions for the content of the introductory sections. Dr. Michael Marquardt, Associate head of International Programs/USDA Graduate School (formerly OEF Director of Human Resources) provided encouragement in the early stages of handbook development. Joan Goodin, OEF Deputy Director, took a keen interest in the handbook and provided the staff resources needed for its completion.

Paddy McLaughlin, Concepts and Design, worked magic in capturing the spirit of the handbook in her design.

And finally, special thanks to OEF Executive Director Elise Smith, who believed in the handbook from start to finish.

Suzanne Kindervatter
Suzanne Kindervatter
Washington, D.C., 1983

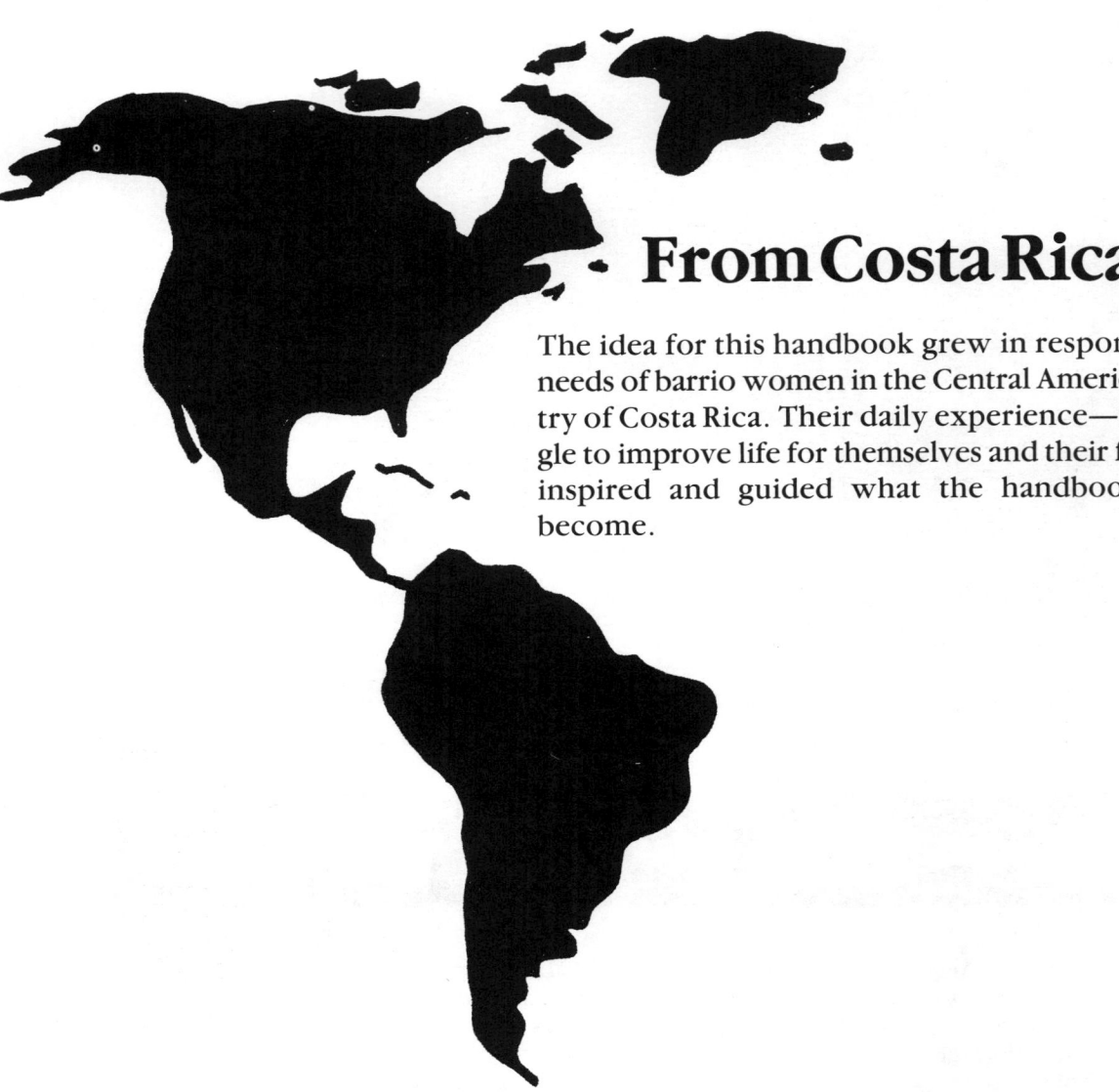

From Costa Rica...

The idea for this handbook grew in response to the needs of barrio women in the Central American country of Costa Rica. Their daily experience—the struggle to improve life for themselves and their families—inspired and guided what the handbook would become.

to Thailand and Honduras...

After a preliminary handbook was written, it travelled to nearby Honduras and across the Pacific Ocean to Thailand in Southeast Asia. Rural women in both places participated in programs based on the handbook activities. They shared their thoughts, their problems, and their hopes. They grew as individuals and as groups able to work together for economic and community improvements. Out of these experiences, the handbook grew into its final form.

Note: Since publication of the original English edition this handbook has been used extensively throughout Africa. A special French edition incorporates visual materials from West Africa.

to you!

And now the handbook comes to you. Use it as a tool for enabling women you know: to organize, to acquire marketable skills, to solve problems. Use it to enable women to reach for their own dreams.

For women, by women: How the handbook developed

The Women in Central America and Southeast Asia have already benefitted from this handbook. They are probably much like women in your locale.

Their days start early and end late. From morning til night, they work hard to care for their families and to bring home resources needed for survival. Some women must walk miles each day for water or for sticks to use as fuel. They may try to grow vegetables in small garden patches, or may spend hours each day travelling to a nearby city to earn enough money for food. Meanwhile, their young children are often home alone. If the children become sick, clinics can be far away and too expensive.

Many women, as sole supporters of their families, shoulder these burdens on their own. Others share responsibilities with husbands or partners, or members of an extended family. Though their individual situations are a bit different, all these women have a common bond. They are vital to the welfare and development of their families and communities.

Picture a village or barrio woman you know. She and others like her want a better life. However, many obstacles stand between them and their goal. Many conditions limit women's own development and their contributions to family and community development. For instance, women typically lack employment and educational opportunities, or access to services such as child care and credit. Their own lack of confidence and the restrictive attitudes of family members may also stand in the way. In addition, discriminative laws keep women from owning property, working certain kinds of jobs, and from earning incomes equal to men.

This handbook was created to enable women to overcome some of these obstacles themselves. Community women and members of private and governmental organizations all helped create the handbook.

From 1977-79, OEF International, then known as the Overseas Education Fund (OEF), a development assistance organization based in Washington, D.C., worked with the *Federación de Organizaciones Voluntarias* (FOV) in Costa Rica on a unique program for women in the barrios of urban San Jose. Through the program, women entered government-sponsored technical training programs and found jobs. They started their own small businesses, began community-based child care, and secured water and electricity for their communities.

The program used a series of "human development activities" to organize women and to involve them in identifying important needs and problems. When the Costa Rican women first began the program, they were reserved and discouraged. After several group meetings, they gained more self-assurance and began to take initiative for improving their lives and their communities.

Some magic seems to happen when women get together to explore their potential and their problems and to plan mutual self-help activities. The women become transformed. They begin by feeling resigned and accepting of their situation—and move to actively attempting to change it.

OEF saw this magic work in Costa Rica and wondered if the approach would be useful for women in other countries. Inspired by the Costa Rica experience, OEF prepared a preliminary handbook that drew on the field of nonformal adult education.

In 1980-81, organizations in Honduras and Thailand used the handbook in their programs with OEF assistance. The *Federación de Asociaciones Femeninas Hondureñas* (FAFH) in Honduras was implementing a legal education program for rural women. They included the handbook as a means to bring women together and to strengthen their abilities to work collectively. In Thailand, the Northeast Regional Training Center (NERTC) (Division of Land Settlements, Department of Public Welfare, Ministry of Interior) was beginning a new program for village women in the Northeast. The aim of this program was to enable women to increase family incomes and to become more involved in village development activities.

The women in both Honduras and Thailand at first had doubts about the programs offered. Promises had been made to them before and not kept. They were unsure of what they would gain. In Thailand, in the very resource-poor Northeast, some of the village women lived with a sense of despair.

What then happened in Honduras and Thailand was like what happened in Costa Rica. During the program, the women realized that they could solve some of their problems, and they actually did so. The Honduran women worked together and successfully won rights to land ownership and access to government services. The Thais began collective small-business activities, including chicken raising, textiles, and pig raising.

Besides these concrete economic benefits, the women felt the program was important to their self-worth. As a number of women in Thailand said, "I became more confident. I'm not afraid now to speak up in meetings and give my ideas."

The programs in Honduras and Thailand helped determine what would be useful and not useful to include in the handbook. Learning from the Honduran and Thai rural women, FAFH, and the NERTC, OEF produced the handbook in final form. Since the handbook was completed, it also has been very successfully used in Ecuador, Morocco, Jordan, Zaire, and Senegal.

The magic that worked in Costa Rica, in Honduras, in Thailand, can work in your locale too. But keep in mind that this handbook is not a solution for all the problems women and their families face. Change must occur on many fronts, from educational institutions to unjust economic structures. This handbook promotes some of the change needed. It enables women to strengthen their faith in themselves and to work together to gain specific economic and social benefits.

One of the staff of the NERTC in Northeastern Thailand very aptly summed up the handbook's meaning:

In our other programs, the villagers have already gained "hammers" and "saws"—certain technical skills they need in their lives. This program is like a "rope," linking them together and helping them to put their skills to effective use.

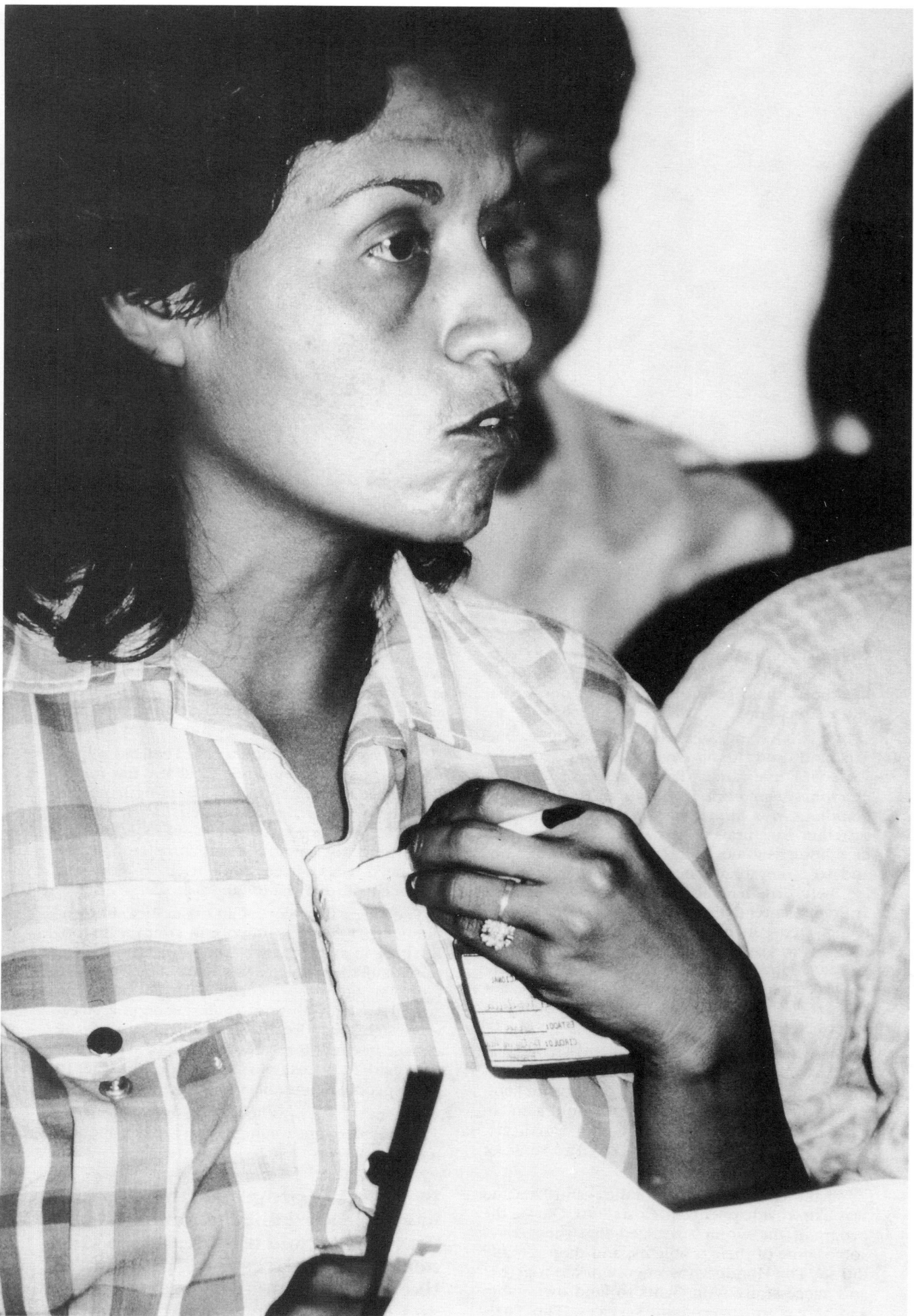

Ideas for using the handbook

This section is your guide for how to use the handbook. Read through the following pages. You will find out what the handbook includes and how it is organized. This section can also help you decide how best to use the handbook for the needs of women in your program.

The handbook is easy to use. The activities and learning materials can all be adapted to fit the culture and situation of your participants. Think of the handbook as a friend who can help groups of women work for change that is important to them.

Promoting women's learning and action groups

What, you must be asking yourself, can using this handbook accomplish? The handbook is a tool for organizing groups of women to identify critical issues and problems in their lives and to do something about them. The groups are called "*learning and actions groups*" because women first think about and discuss their problems and then actually work together to solve them.

Different groups of women will decide to take different kinds of action. For example, many women may be interested in improving their abilities to earn money and will seek technical training or start a cooperative business. Finding sources of credit is another possibility. Other women may be concerned about family and community problems. They may decide to set up cooperative child care or to contact local authorities about improving transportation to a nearby town. The possibilites are up to the women themselves.

To aid in planning, here are some other questions that have been asked about using the handbook and the answers to those questions:

What are some benefits women can gain from the handbook program?

- Increased family income, by finding profitable kinds of work
- Solutions to community problems, such as lack of electricity
- Knowledge of community resources and how to use them
- Greater self-respect and confidence
- Ability to make a plan and carry it out
- Knowledge of legal rights
- Strengthened ability to work together as a group.

Who can participate in a program that uses the handbook?

The handbook was designed for women who live in the same community, whether urban barrio or rural village. Age makes no difference. It can be used with groups of women who have considerable education or with groups who don't know how to read and write.

The handbook was developed for women's groups, but it has also been used effectively with groups of men and women together and groups of only men. The handbook can be adapted for these groups by changing some of the visual aids and stories used in the activities.

For what kinds of programs will the handbook be useful?

The handbook can make an important contribution to many different kinds of development efforts:

- In **small business enterprise or job placement programs,** the handbook enables women to determine the profitability of different work options and to remove obstacles—such as lack of child care or credit—that prevent them from gaining full economic benefits;
- In **technical skills training programs**, the handbook can help prepare women for skills training, by building confidence and encouraging them to consider non-traditional kinds of work;
- In **community development programs,** the handbook helps women identify needs, organize, and work together;
- In **programs emphasizing water, health, or other areas,** the handbook involves women in defining problems from their own perspectives and motivates women to solve them; • In **almost any kind of program**, the handbook promotes a sense of self-worth and a spirit of community self-reliance.

Who can coordinate or "lead" the learning and action groups?

The group leader or coordinator can be a group member or someone from outside the group. The coordinator needs reading and writing skills. She especially needs to have faith in the group members.

The coordinator can be: a government extension worker, a local midwife, or a respected village woman. Community women themselves are often the best coordinators. They may need to have training and guidance in using the handbook provided by a private or government development organization.

Fitting the handbook to specific women's needs

Take a look at the "Table of contents" inside the front cover. You will see that the handbook includes eight topics important to women:

Getting Together
Women Themselves
Women and Work
Working Together
Women and Their Families
Organizing for Community Problem Solving
Women's
Rights From Learning Group to Action Group

For each of these topics, there are several meetings. In the handbook, the meetings include guidelines for discussion and visual aids that help groups of women to identify issues that concern them. It takes about two hours to finish a meeting. Two hours is an average time. Some groups may need more time and others may need less.

Women's needs and interests differ from place to place. The handbook is flexible. It can fit the specific needs of women in your program.

There are several ways to use the handbook in order to match the needs of a particular group of women.

- One way to use the handbook is to follow the eight topics and eighteen meetings in the order of the "table of contents." If women meet once a week for two hours, this would take 18 weeks. It is best to allow about a week between meetings. Then women have time to work on development activities between each meeting. Using all the meetings in the handbook gives women the opportunity to deal with many different issues of personal, economic, and community development.
- A second way to use the handbook is to include all eight topics and eighteen meetings but to change their order. For instance, women in your locale may have a special interest in *Women and Work* or *Women's Rights*. These topics could then be used earlier in the program. However, it's probably best not to change the order of the first and last meetings. *Getting Together* is an introduction to the program, and *From Learning Group to Action Group* helps the women plan on-going activities.
- A third way to use the handbook is to choose only some of the topics and meetings. For example, if women are especially interested in community development, you may only want to use two topics: *Working Together* and *Organizing for Community Problem Solving*. You can use any topic alone or any combination of topics—depending on the specific needs of women in your program. There is one disadvantage, though, to only using some of the topics. The women miss the chance to consider the importance of other concerns in their lives.

No matter how you decide to use the handbook, there are some things you can do that will help make a good program. Think about these tips when you plan your program.

Tips for a good program

1. Include between 10-20 women in your learning and action group.
2. Hold meetings at a time and place convenient for the women.
3. Schedule the meetings a few days or one week apart, so women have time to think about and act on what they've discussed.
4. Have two "leaders" or coordinators for each group.
5. If the coordinators are not community women themselves, have one or two local women be assistant coordinators. They can help arrange the meetings and lead the discussions. This prepares them to help the group plan on-going activities after the last meeting.

"Facilitating," not teaching

The Thais used the term "tham sadùak"—to make easy—for "facilitate." And that gives a pretty good sense of what "facilitating" is all about.

How are a teacher and facilitator different? Remember back to some of your experiences in school. If your experience was typical, the teacher usually stood in front of the classroom and lectured about information the students needed to memorize. That approach can work with children. But lecturing can be ineffective with adults, particularly if the goal of a program is problem solving and group action. A facilitator respects the knowledge and experience adults have. She helps other women feel comfortable about expressing their ideas and discussing problems from their own point of view.

The coordinator or leader for the women's learning and action group meetings can be thought of as a "facilitator." What does this mean? First, it means that the coordinator makes the meeting place comfortable and arranges it so that the women can sit informally in a circle. Second, during the meeting, the coordinator asks questions and poses problems for the women to analyze. She gives her own opinion about a topic and listens with respect to the opinions of others. Third, she guides the women from discussion to action, by helping the women themselves decide what they want to do about a certain issue or problem.

Facilitating means searching and discovering, not giving answers or telling women what they should do. It's about women choosing a course of action themselves. In the meetings, there can be no real expert on the challenges women face—except the women themselves!

Conducting a group meeting

Once you've decided on the participants, coordinators, and topics for your program, you can start preparing for the group meetings. The eighteen handbook meetings include specific guidelines for a coordinator to use in conducting a group meeting. Each meeting is made up of one or more activities. All the activities have the same format.

As an example, turn to Meeting 3, "*Setting Our Goals*" (p. 33). This meeting has two parts or activities, "What is a goal?" and "Deciding on a Personal Goal." In both these activities, there are four sections: purpose, materials, steps, and ideas to take home.

The **purpose** explains why an activity is included and what it will accomplish. **Materials** lists the audio-visual aids that are needed for the meeting. There are three kinds of materials that may be needed: 1) supplies, such as newsprint and felt tip pens, that the coordinator should have on hand; 2) materials that are included in the handbook and can be used as is, such as stories or skits; and 3) materials that need to be prepared by the coordinator using samples in the handbook as a guide, such as posters, puppets, and photographs.

Steps is the sequence of things the group will do during the meeting. The "Steps" also includes some discussion questions. The fourth section, **ideas to take home**, suggests some ways to end a particular activity.

The real key to conducting a lively, effective group meeting is good preparation. Experienced coordinators, such as community development workers, should read through the activities before a meeting and get needed materials together. Less experienced coordinators, such as community women, may need a structured training program as preparation. The training approach used in Thailand, described in the box, might also be useful for training coordinators for your program.

Suggestions for coordinator training

In Thailand, village women with limited reading and writing abilities were the group coordinators or leaders. Before the village groups started meeting, the leaders attended a two-week training program on how to use the hendbook. During the training, the leaders participated in all the handbook meetings, from number one to eighteen. Teams of leaders practiced facilitating different meetings, under the guidance of staff of a government training center.

The two-week training gave the leaders basic skills for using the handbook. Then, after the group meeting began, the coordinators met weekly to review each upcoming meeting. The weekly review was attended by two staff members of the training center. It helped the women remember what to do in each meeting.

The combination of structured training and support from experienced trainers worked well for preparing coordinators in the Thai program.

And finally, evaluating

When your program is underway, you may begin to wonder: How are the women reacting to the program? Are there ways the program can be better? What are the program results and accomplishments??

To help you answer such questions, here are some simple ideas for how to evaluate your program. Sometimes we think of evaluation as an outside judgment of something we've done. But here, evaluation means looking ourselves at what we've done and thinking about how to make it even better. The following methods can be used in your program.

After a meeting—The women in your program will probably have some ideas about what they like and don't like about it. Many times, their ideas can strengthen the program. To find out what the women think, ask them a simple question at the end of a meeting, such as:

- What did you think about the meeting?
- What was good about the meeting? What could be better next time?
- What one word describes your thoughts about today's meeting?

For coordinators—The program coordinators may be interested in a way to improve their skills. One way is to use the "facilitator skills development form" on the following page. The form can be used by teams of coordinators. They don't need to show them to anyone else.

At the end of the program—When we give time and care to a program, it's natural to want to know the results. Some outcomes, like newly formed small businesses, are easy to observe. Other possible changes, like women's attitudes or how a business affects a family, may not be as obvious. To identify these kinds of changes, a questionnaire can be useful. The questionnaire can be used only at the end of a program, or at both the beginning and end to determine specific changes. The sample questionnaire at the end of this section might be helpful for your program evaluation.

A note about newsprint

Many of the handbook activities use "newsprint and felt tip pens." Newsprint is the paper newspapers are printed on. In the activities, it is taped to the wall and used for writing or drawing.

Newsprint is inexpensive and comes in large sheets—60 cm x 90 cm or larger (about 2 ft. by 3 ft.). You can usually buy blank sheets of newsprint at an agency that prints a newspaper. Sometimes you can buy it at school supply stores.

If you cannot find newsprint, then use other large sheets of paper or a blackboard.

Facilitator skills development form

Meeting/Date _____

Directions: After each meeting, take a few minutes to complete this form. Then, discuss your answers with your partner. Give each other suggestions on how to do better in the areas you select. This quick and easy form will help you become an outstanding facilitator!

How did the participants react to the session? How did I feel about the session—and why?	What did I do well?
What difficulties or problems occurred? Why?	What areas would I like to do better in next time? ☐ arranging the meeting (chairs in a circle, places for small groups, etc.) ☐ preparing supplies in advance ☐ preparing audio-visual materials in advance ☐ giving instructions ☐ giving a "mini-lecture" ☐ using a particular audio-visual material ☐ asking questions which promote discussion ☐ coordinating tasks with partner ☐ guiding participants to discover answers, not giving them answers ☐ other, specifically:

Finding out program results
(A sample questionnaire)

NOTE: These are questions that can be asked to women who have attended the learning and action group meetings.

1. Why did you attend the program?

2. What did you like about the program? How did it help you?

3. What did you not like about the program? How should it be changed?

4. What goal did you set in the program? What are you doing to achieve it?

5. What community problems did your group decide to solve? What have you done together to solve the problems?

6. What other activities has your group done together?

7. As a result of the program, what specifically have you done to:
   a. increase your family income? (if a woman has actually earned more money, how much has been earned?)

   b. save or borrow money? (if money has been saved or borrowed, how much? how has the woman used the money?)

   c. improve family relationships?

   d. solve community problems?

   e. make other changes to improve your life or your community?

8. How many meetings did you attend? If you did not attend all the meetings, why not?

Getting together

This section includes ideas for contacting women about your program and guidelines for the first "learning and action group" meeting.

The first meeting sets the mood for the program. Women have the opportunity to talk about what's important to them. No one tells them what they should or shouldn't think or do.

During the meeting, women get better acquainted with each other. Then, they find out more about what the program has to offer by listening to a letter written by a woman from Central America. Finally, they discuss what they expect from the program and what they hope to gain.

Before the first meeting

The first step in organizing a "learning and action group" is contacting women who might participate. How can you find these women? And, what should you tell them about your program?

Making contact

There is no one best way to make contact with women in your community. Here are some ways from Thailand and Central America that might be useful in your locale.

Making contact

At a community meeting— a good opportunity to let women—and men—know about the program

Through leaders— village heads, community leaders, can be good "go-betweens"

Publicity— posters, loud speakers, local radio shows

And— what are your ideas???

At a party— an annual or specially planned celebration can bring women together

Visits— from house to house or at a place, like a well, where women congregate

Through an organization— local, respected organizations can sponsor the program for members

What to say

Once you have gotten some women together, what might you say? Think about why women in your locale would be interested in a development program. Women are likely to attend if they can see how a program fits their needs. Women may have attended other programs in the past and found them a waste of time. They may have doubts about what you're offering. The women need to know how your program will benefit them. They also need to know that meetings will be held at a time and place that fits with their busy schedules.

A good way to begin is to talk with women about what the results of the program can be. The program can help them take action to increase their family incomes. It will enable them to work together to improve their communities. It can also be a way to find out about the law and their rights. For more ideas on the benefits of the program, read about what's happened to other women who've participated. This information is included in the earlier section, "*Ideas for Using the Handbook*" (pp. 11-17) and in the "*Letter from Maria*" in Meeting #1 (p. 25).

Talk with women about what's important to them. The program, any program, can't do everything. You can help the women identify the ways the program does match with their needs.

Solving problems that arise

After your program begins, some women may not want to continue to attend. Problems can occur. In one case, husbands objected to their wives' participation. In another, women themselves became confused about the purpose of the program. In Central America and Thailand, these problems were solved. Special meetings were held to answer questions and to talk about what had happened. This cleared up the difficulties.

What's most important to remember—from beginning to end—is this. *Listen* to the women . . . . . and they'll guide the way.

Getting to know each other and the program

Getting acquainted (about 1 hour)

Purpose
The first part of Meeting 1 helps participants know one another and the facilitators. It also sets the tone of the entire program. In most meetings participants will sit in a circle and share their ideas. The facilitators will serve as guides for what to do and discuss.

Materials
Music (tape or record), if available

Small "objects," such as flowers, stars, or animals cut from colored paper (see sample on page 23). (Count the number of participants and facilitators in your program and divide by two. This is the number of objects you will need. Cut two of each object, and three of one of the objects if you have an odd number of participants and facilitators.)

A box or basket from which the paper cut-outs can be selected

Steps

1. Before this first meeting, think about how the women you've contacted feel about coming. Do the women know each other? Have they attended other kinds of meetings before? Will they feel shy or distrustful? It's natural for the women to feel some hesitation about the meeting.

    So, how can you help them feel comfortable? Think about how to make your meeting room friendly and warm. You might have music playing and some decorations, such as posters on the walls or flowers. Refreshments can be a good idea too.

    When the participants finally arrive, welcome them warmly. Sit together in a circle. Remember—if the women feel comfortable, they will be more likely to come to other meetings.

2. After everyone is seated in the circle, explain that the purpose of the meeting is to get to know something about each other and about the program. Ask if there are any questions. Now, you're ready to start.

3. Have each participant and facilitator select a paper cut-out from the box or basket. Then, tell everyone to find a partner by matching objects. When all have found their partners, explain that they will have twenty minutes to interview each other. After the interviews, they will introduce their partners to the entire group. In the interviews, the partners should ask each other these questions (or three other questions you choose yourself):
    - What would you like to have the participants know about you?
    - What did you do yesterday?
    - What was an especially happy event in your life?

4. Have the pairs do their interviews (20 minutes).

5. Get the group back together and go around the circle having partners introduce each other. Partners will tend to tell more than if a woman introduced herself.

6. Take a five minute break before the next part of this meeting.

What is the program about? (1 hour)

Purpose
The participants have gotten to know each other a bit. Now they can look at the program and what they can expect to gain from it. In this activity, a participant from another program "speaks" to the group through a letter. She shares her feelings about the program and what she gained from it. Besides needing to feel comfortable, the women will come to future meetings if they believe they will benefit from them. The letter gives examples of the kind of benefits the women can expect.

Materials
Photo and "Letter" from a previous participant/Use photo and letter on pages 24 and 25.
  (For literate groups, you can give a copy of the letter to all the participants)
Refreshments (for after the activity), if available

Steps

1. Put the photo in a place where it can be seen by everyone. Tell the participants that the woman in the picture attended a program similar to theirs in another country. She has written a letter to them about her experiences. Read the letter to the participants. Pass out copies in a literate group so members can read along.

2. After you have read the letter aloud, divide the participants into groups of five or six members for discussion. You should not join one of these groups during the discussion, because you will visit each group.

3. Explain that the small groups will have about 20 minutes to discuss three questions. After this, a member of each group will report on the discussion to the entire group.

   The discussion questions are:
   - What did you think of the letter?
   - Why did you come today?
   - What do you hope to get out of the program?

4. To make sure that the groups talk about all the questions, ask the groups to move on to the second question after about 5 minutes and the third question after about 10 minutes. Participants may need your encouragement to talk about their expectations of the program. Visit each of the groups. Promote discussion by asking individuals to respond to the three questions or by asking other related questions.

5. After the groups have discussed the three questions ask one member of each group to report.

Ideas to take home
To end the meeting, talk with the participants about how their expectations can be met by the program. Be clear about what the program can do and can't do. (See "Ideas for Using the Handbook", pp. 11-17, for information.)

  You will need to respond to the participants' discussion in their groups. Explain what the program includes. Stress what the benefits can be for women who attend.

  Before closing, ask if there are any questions. Also, decide with the participants a convenient time and place for the next meeting.

  End the first session with refreshments—another opportunity for the participants to become better acquainted and to feel motivated to attend the next session!

Materials 1

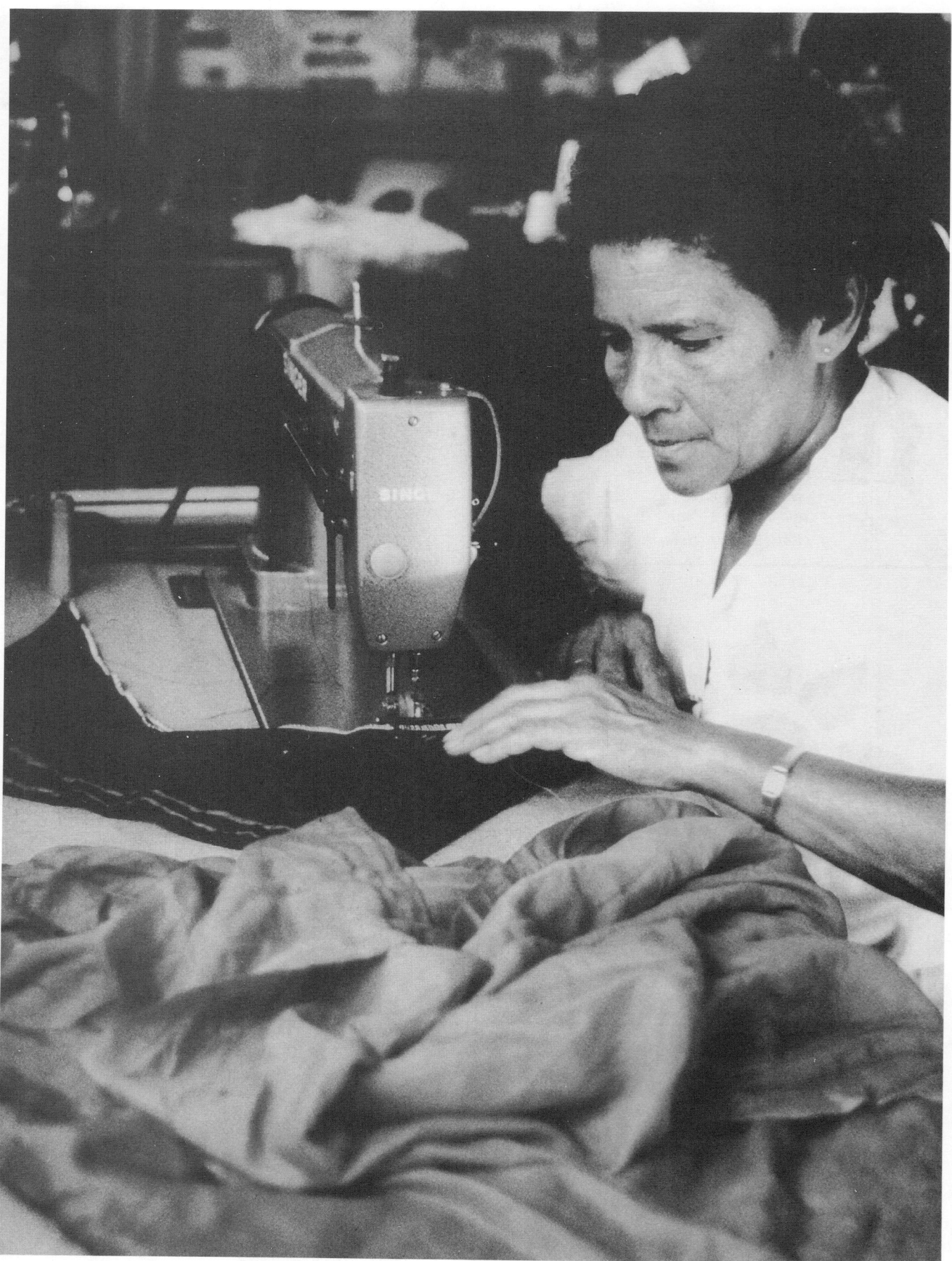

Letter from a friend

Dear Friend

My name is Maria, and I live in a country called Costa Rica.

Not long ago, I came to a meeting like your meeting here today. The women who invited us to attend were members of a community organization. They encouraged us to join a program which would help us improve our lives. I did join. I attended the program meetings. Let me tell you about the wonderful things that happened because of the program!

Before the program, I didn't know what to do about my problems. Everyday, I got up and took some vegetables to the market to sell. When I came home, there was always so much to do for my family. I felt tired and worried about many things. I had no idea that I—along with others—could change the situation.

When I was invited to attend the meeting about the program, I was hesitant. I thought it might be a waste of time. I was curious, though. So, I went. At the first meeting, I heard that the program could help us achieve goals and solve problems. I didn't understand all this. But I was interested to find out more.

The first few meetings didn't have many participants—only I and about six other women from my community. When others saw that the program as something special, more joined. At first, some husbands didn't want their wives involved. But, when they saw their wives change, they gave their support.

In the meetings, we played games and heard stories. It was fun! At the same time, we learned so much. And we did things together to improve our lives.

I gained so much from the program. I'd like you to know some of the benefits. At the start, we realized that we had a common problem. When we attended the meetings or were away from home, we had no one to look after our children. So, we organized a community child care center. I'm glad to have this center we all can use. Next, we realized we shared another problem—too little income. Together, we found a way to learn sewing and dressmaking. Then, we decided we didn't want to work away from home, so we thought of setting up a sewing cooperative. We contacted an expert on coops who's helping us now to get started. We'll need to build a coop workshop too. Working together, we also have gotten water and electricty for part of the community, and we're obtaining ownership rights to our land. Of course, not everything has gone smoothly, but that doesn't make us discouraged.

The program made us confident of our abilities and of what we can do working together. We learned how to get along. We learned how to analyze problems and how to find solutions ourselves. We found out about community resources and about our rights. I even share some responsibilities now at home with my husband!

Before, I didn't have any of these things and I didn't know how to get them. I didn't know I had the qualities that today I've discovered in myself. That's why I feel so happy now—because I feel I have value as a person.

Your friend

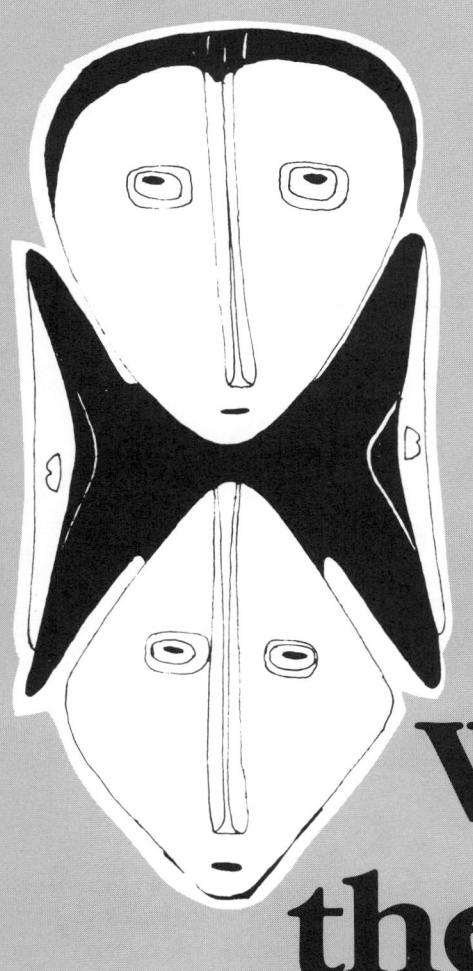

Women themselves

In many settings, women do not appreciate their strengths. The three meetings in this section enable women to realize their abilities to change aspects of their situations and to make plans to do so. The meetings help build confidence and women's respect for themselves and each other.

After talking about their own lives in Meeting 2, the women then discuss personal goals. In Meeting 3, they identify a goal they'd like to achieve, such as starting a small business or producing more food for the family. The women also learn a goal-setting method they can use on their own.

Meeting 4 enables the women to make plans and find resources to reach the goals they've set.

Who am I? (30 minutes)

Purpose
There are three activities in this meeting. Each one helps to promote the participants' self-awareness and confidence in expressing themselves. In many of the later meetings, participants will think about and plan for change in their own lives and their communities. This meeting helps the participants to know themselves better and what's important to them. In the first activity, they identify many different parts of themselves or "roles."

Materials
Newsprint and felt tip pens (or blackboard and chalk)

Steps

1. To start, explain to the participants that they will be thinking about themselves and what's important to them. We need to know ourselves before we can solve our problems.

2. Tell the women that they are going to play a game called "Who Am I?".

3. Divide the women into groups of five or six members. Meet separately with each group and instruct the group to think of all the possible things they *are*. Explain that the teams will then compete to see which team thought of the most. Take about 5 minutes for this step. (Some examples of "Who Am I?" are: mother, wife, sister, teacher, nurse, aunt, member of a certain association, farmer, seller, etc. The responses do not have to be formal jobs, but *roles* that the women have in their lives.)

4. Bring the teams back together. Put up sheets of newsprint. Explain that each team will alternate in giving an answer to "Who Am I?". All the members of all the teams should have a chance to respond.

5. Now, start with the first member of the first team, and write her answer on the paper. For preliterate groups, draw a stock figure or symbol. (Note: To increase excitement, each item can be on only one list!)

6. Record the responses of a member of each team in turn. After all have responded, begin again with the first person. When the teams have no more answers, the team with the longest newsprint list is the "winner." But—explain that they're all really "winners." They had a good time and found out more about themselves!

7. Your job in the discussion is to guide the participants in examining what they do and how they live. Here are some questions to use:
   - Which of these parts of yourself or "roles" did you choose yourself? Which was in some way given to you?
   - What are some of the things you do in your different roles?
   - Which roles do you like? Why? Which don't you like? Why not? Could you change these things?
   - Are there some things that you would like to do or be that are not on the lists? How could you do or be these things?

Ideas to take home
Participants should end this activity feeling an appreciation for the many things they are and do. Show your appreciation for the women and their different roles too. Also, point out to them the roles they chose themselves. There are some areas in which they have choice in their lives.

Take a five minute break.

Looking at what we do and think

2

What are some of my values?
(30 minutes)

Purpose
In this activity, the participants will discover some things that they like and that are important to them. They will also have a chance to see that these things are different for different people.

Materials
"My Values" Questions/Use questions on page 32 (For literate groups, give a copy of questions to each participant)

Steps
1. It's important to explain to the women that there are no right and wrong answers in this activity. We're all different. We need to understand and respect each other's differences.
2. Read the first question and ask for volunteers to respond. Call on about five women who want to give answers. (As an alternative, you can give all the participants a chance to respond to each of the questions. This will take more time.)
3. Go through each of the questions in the same way as the first question. It's not necessary to write down the answers.
4. For discussion, use questions like these:
   - Which questions were easy to answer? Why? Which were difficult?
   - What did you learn about yourself that you didn't know before?

Ideas to take home
To close this activity, note that everyone expressed her own likes and opinions. The different ideas weren't right or wrong. Different things are important to different people. Usually, we can get along with each other better if we try to understand these differences.

Take a few minutes break.

Seeing the same thing differently
(1 hour)

Purpose
In the last part of this meeting, participants look at a common problem situation in their lives. The activity helps them see that people may see a problem in different ways. These views are important to know in trying to find ways to solve a problem.

Materials
A set of "Story Cards" for each group of five or six participants
Make your own using the sample on page 31 as a guide (Mount the cards on cardboard, if possible, and cut out each card so it is separate.)

Steps
1. Divide the participants into groups of five or six members. Give each group a set of "story cards" (make sure the cards are shuffled).

2. Tell the groups they will have 20 minutes to make up a story by putting the cards in the order they choose. Emphasize that there is no right or wrong story. Encourage the groups to be creative. Also, explain that the story should be something that could really happen in a community in their country.

3. Have the small groups meet for 20 minutes, then present their stories.

4. The discussion with the entire group looks at the stories created by the participants. Focus on how the stories relate to situations in their own lives. Discussion questions:
    - How were the stories different? How were they similar?
    - What parts of the stories do you think are most true? Can you think of similar things that happened to members of your own family or friends?
    - Each group was given the same set of cards. Why weren't all the stories the same? (Draw out some reasons by asking other questions if necessary.)
    - Does this ever happen in our own lives—we all see the same thing, but we see it differently? Can you think of any situations you've been in where this happened? (Give ideas for situations if the participants have difficulty: family disagreements, conflicts with neighbors, differences of opinion with a friend, different views given at a community meeting, and so on.)
    - Did your initial idea of the story change as members of your group added their ideas? How do our own ideas change in our lives as we get new information?

5. Point out that we all have different points of view. We need to try to understand and respect—rather than criticize—how other people think and feel. This is important if we want to work together successfully.

Ideas to take home
Before ending, go around the circle and have each participant complete this statement:
   In our meeting today, the most important thing I realized was...

Materials 2

From United Nations materials

"My Values" Questions

1. What is your favorite food?

2. What is something you love to do?

3. What is one thing you want to change in your neighborhood?

4. What qualities do you want in a friend?

5. What makes you happy?

6. What is the most important thing you want your children to remember?

7. What is the one thing you hope your children will not have to go through?

8. What makes you angry?

9. What are the qualities of a good husband?

10. If you found ($10), how would you spend it?

11. What is something you did to help someone?

12. What would you say if you met the leader of your country?

Adapted from: *Values Clarification: A Handbook of Practical Strategies for Teachers and Students* by Sidney B. Simon, Leland W. Howe, and Howard Kirschenbaum, (New York: Hart Publishing Co., Inc. 1972).

Setting our goals 3

What is a goal? (about 1 hour)

Purpose
In the first part of this meeting, participants will learn what a "goal" is. Then, they will be ready to decide on personal goals for themselves later in the meeting.

Materials
Happy and Unhappy Woman Posters/Make your own using samples on pages 36-39
"Clear goal" and "Unclear goal" stories/Use stories on pages 36-37
"Clear goal" and "Unclear goal" game/Use game on page 35

Steps

1. Two things are important to remember in this meeting. First, the idea of a "goal" may be very new to some of the participants. Because their lives have been difficult, they may need time to understand—and especially to believe—that they can bring about change themselves. Be encouraging. If you really believe in the potential of the women in your group, they will too.

   Here is the second thing to remember. You can best help the participants to understand a "goal" and to gain confidence if you share your own experience. Talk about a goal in your own life. It will also promote greater trust between you and the participants.

2. To help the women feel comfortable, begin with a short "warm-up." The warm-up could be a quick game (such as recalling everyone's name) or a song.

3. After the warm-up, explain that this session will be about "goals" in our lives. Ask participants for their ideas about what a goal is.

4. When several have given their ideas, talk about how we can know something is a goal. Explain that a goal is something:
   - we want to do
   - we think is an improvement
   - we are willing to work toward

   Then, talk about a goal you have in your own life. Your goal might be something you want to become, learn, or do better, such as get a new job or gain skills to fix your bicycle. Explain: why you chose it; why it is important to you; how you feel about it. Ask the women if they have any questions.

5. Next, point out that it's important for our goals to be clear. "Clear" means that the goal describes what, how, and when. For example, "I will raise chickens with a loan from the bank within the next four months." Read the "clear goal" and the "unclear goal" stories. Show the drawings that go with them. Ask participants to choose which goal story was clear and which was unclear. Explain again what a "clear goal" means.

6. Play the "Clear goal"/"Unclear goal" game on page 35.

Ideas to take home
Remind participants of what a goal is and that it is important to have clear goals. To end the activity, go quickly around the circle and have participants answer:
- What have I learned about goals?

Take a short break.

Deciding on a personal goal (1 hour)

Purpose
The first part of this meeting focused on the meaning of a *personal goal*. Now participants will identify a goal they would like to achieve.

Materials
Cassette tape recorder and blank tape, if available.
10 cm. diameter (4-in.) cardboard circles for making name tags
Supplies for making name tags: colored paper, felt tip pens, old magazines, and so on
Sample name tag, if available

Steps

1. Remind the participants that they have thought about "goals." Now, it's time for everyone to choose her own goal.

2. Explain that before choosing a clear goal, it helps to think of what we hope our life will be like in the future. Show the participants the cassette recorder and how it works. Explain that everyone will talk on the tape, and then it will be played back. The tape is used for two reasons. First, participants can gain more confidence if they hear their own words on tape. Second, the tape enables the women to hear the "good futures" ideas for a second time. This helps them think more about a possible goal for themselves.

3. If no tape recorder is available, you can still do the activity. Just skip Step #5.

4. Tell the participants to think about how they would like their lives to be five years from now. Then, pass the recorder around the circle and have each participant describe her "good future" dream. The participants may be hesitant to use the tape at first. Encourage them and coach them on their stories: where will you live? what will the house be like? who will you be with? what will you be doing? how will you feel? etc. Without a recorder, just have each woman tell her story in turn.

5. After everyone has recorded her "good future" story, play back the tape.

6. Now have the participants go to separate places in the room. This separation will help them think about their own goals. Explain that it's now time to choose a goal. Say that you'd like everyone to choose a goal that can be achieved by the end of the program (a few months). The "good future" stories on the tape are "long-term" goals. We need to have many "short-term" goals to reach the long-term goals. Participants should choose a short-term goal. Remind them that the goal should be clear. Ask participants to close their eyes and think of a goal they'd like to choose. Allow a few minutes.

7. When all are ready with their goals, ask them to meet in pairs and tell their goals to their partners. Make sure it is short-term and clear. Visit each pair to hear the goals chosen. If participants have not identified a goal or have not made the goal short-term and clear, help them to do so.

8. Participants will now make a "goal name tag." Show them the supplies and explain that they can make any design they want. A design should represent their goal. Partners can help each other make the designs. If you show a sample name tag, this task will be easier for the participants.

9. Bring the participants back together in the circle. Ask each to show her name tag, explain her goal, and why she chose it. After everyone speaks, explain that the next meeting will help everyone achieve her goals.

Ideas to take home
Encourage the women to feel pride and a sense of accomplishment. They've chosen goals that are important to them, and that the program can help them to reach.

Collect the name tags and save them for other meetings.

Materials 3

"Clear or Unclear" game

Instructions: Read each statement. Ask those who think the goal is clear to raise their hands. Then ask those who think the goal is unclear to raise their hands. Talk briefly about why the goal is clear or unclear. For unclear goals, ask the participants to restate them as clear goals. Read all the statements one at a time.

1. (Name) wants the people in her community to work together. (Unclear)
2. (Name) would like to have a better life. (Unclear)
3. (Name) would like her children to complete primary school. (Clear)
4. (Name) would like to repair her house with her friends' help by next July. (Clear)
5. (Name) wants her local officials to help the people more. (Unclear)
6. (Name) wants to work with community members to get running water in the next few months. (Clear)
7. (Name) wants her local officials to create a community recreation center this year. (Clear)
8. (Name) wants more money. (Unclear)
9. (Name) wants to take a course in electrical repair next month so she can find a better paying job as soon as possible. (Clear)
10. (Name) wants herself and her family to be happy. (Unclear)

Remember:
A clear goal includes
what
how and
when!

35

Unclear goal story

(use "unhappy woman" poster with this story)

(Local woman's name) wanted to be a better farmer. She wasn't sure what would make her better, but she tried many things. When (name) planted her crops, she used a lot of fertilizer she found in a local store. When the plants were growing, she gave them lots of water. She also sprayed the plants with an insecticide.

With all she'd done, (name) was anxious for the harvest to come. But, when the time finally arrived, she was shocked to discover the yield was lower than the previous year! (Name) was distressed. She thought she'd done all the things that a good farmer needs to do.

"What had she done wrong?" she wondered.

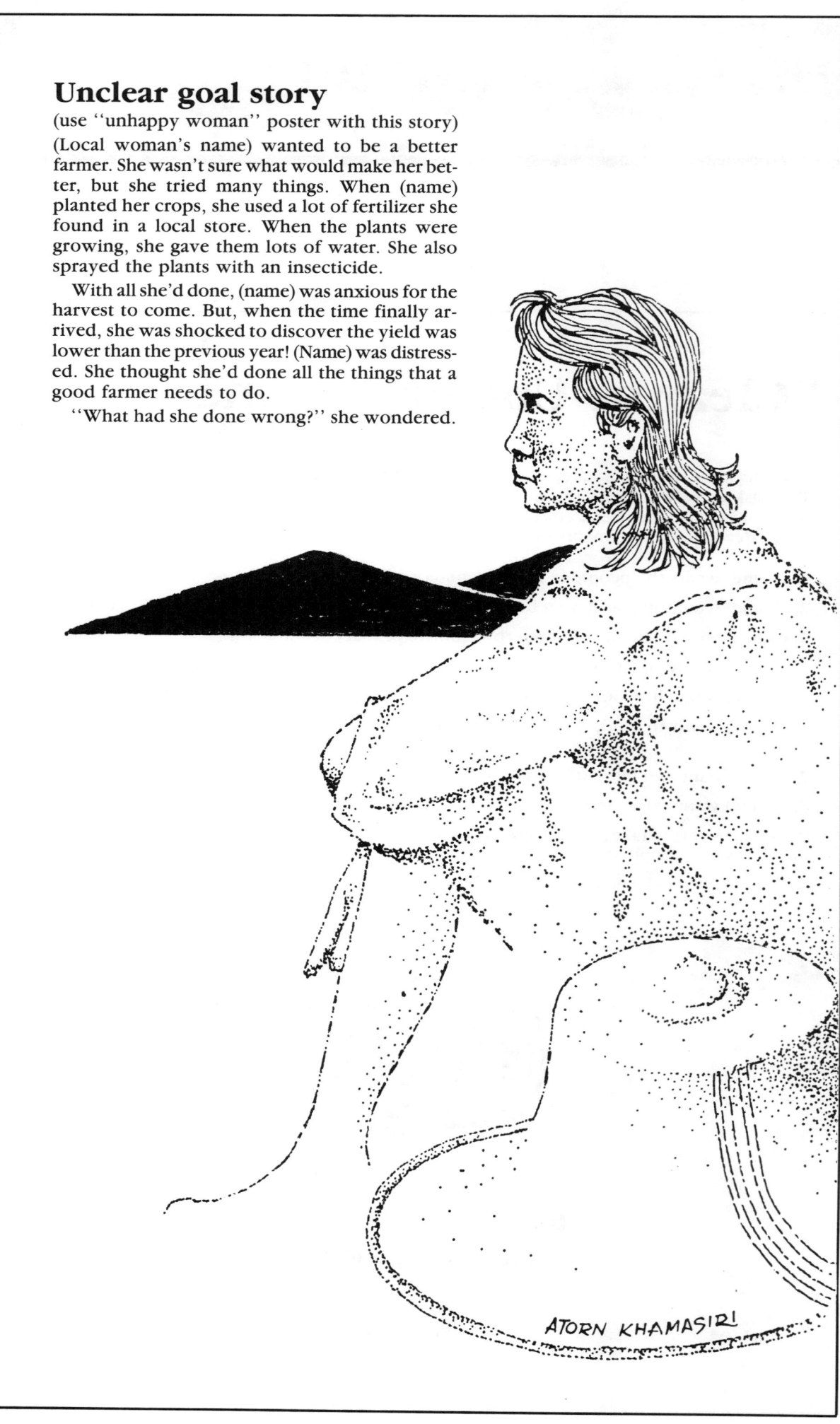

Clear goal story

(use "happy woman" poster with this story)

(Another local name) wanted to produce a higher crop yield next season. She talked to some successful farmers in her community about what helped them to be productive. She also visited the local agriculture extension agent for advice.

(Name) found out that her soil had been planted for too many years with one crop, so she decided to plant another. She also found out what kind of fertilizer the new crop needed and how much water.

At harvest-time, (name) was so happy. She had one of the highest crop yields in her community!

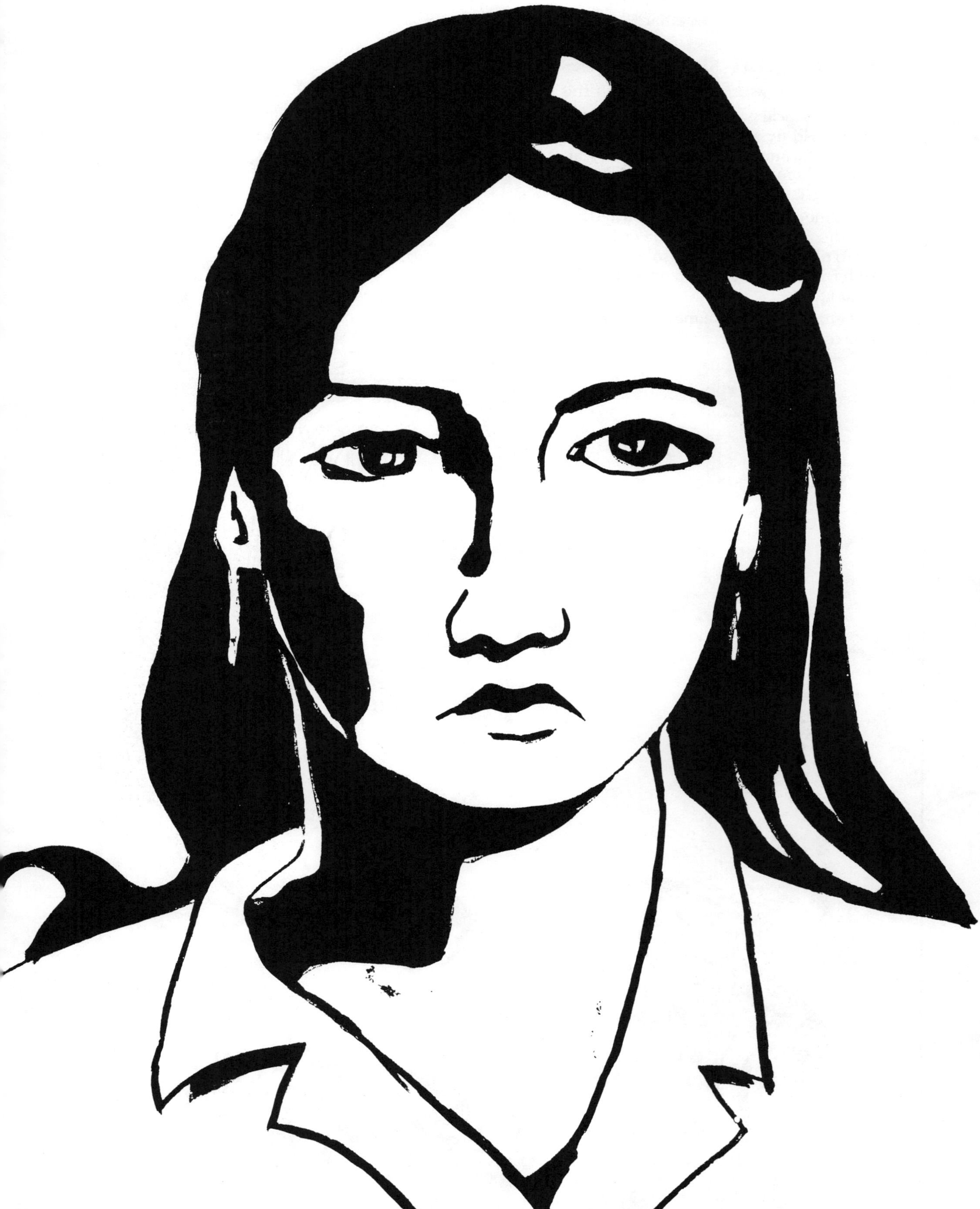

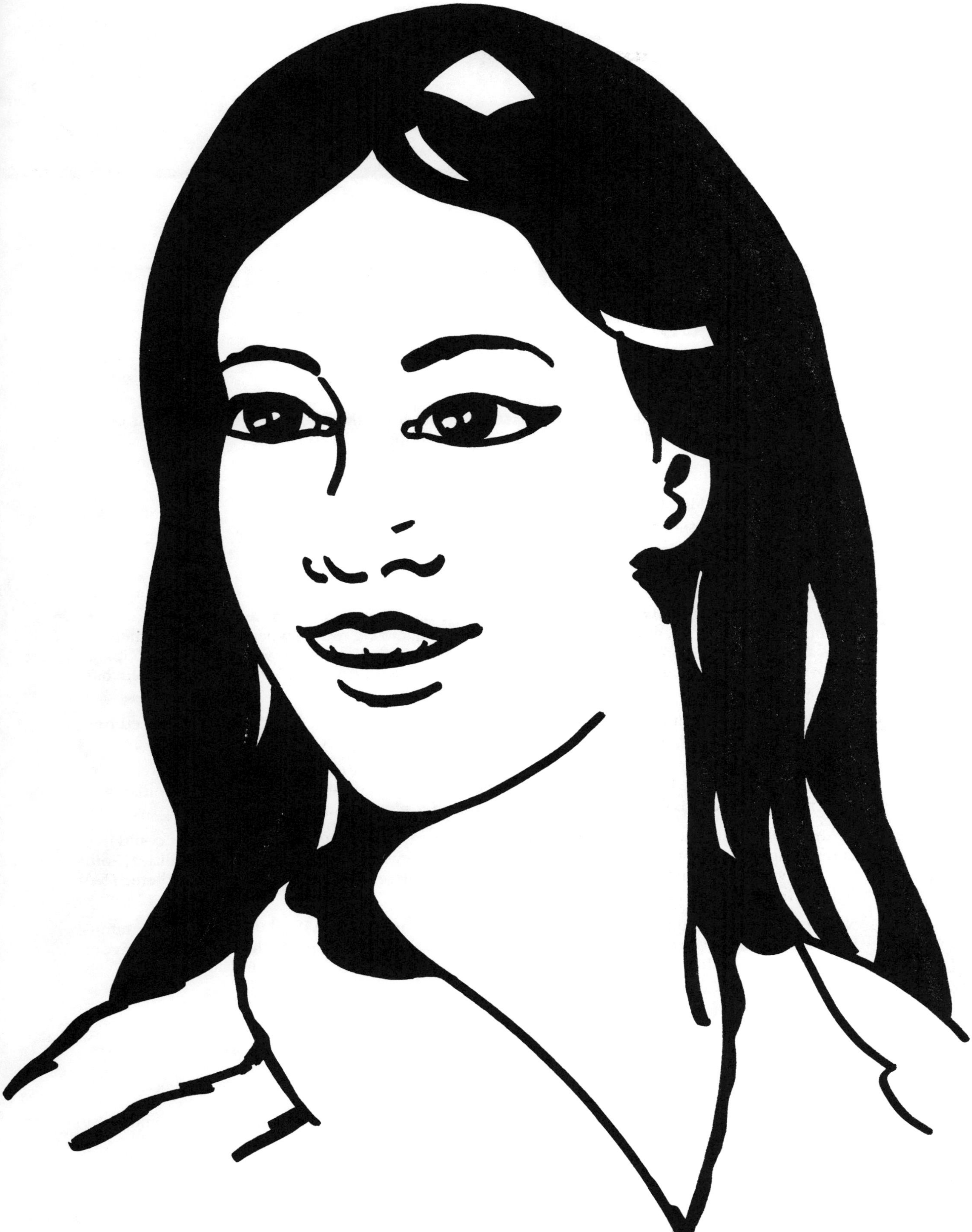

Using personal and community resources (1 hour)

Purpose
In the previous meeting, participants chose personal goals. Now, they plan how to reach their goals. In this activity, the women will identify resources that can be useful to them.

Materials
Goal Name Tags/From Meeting 3
Flannelboard and figures/Make your own using isntructions and samples on pages 42-45
"Using Community Resources" story/Use story provided on page 45

Steps

1. Begin with a warm-up. Mix the goal name tags. Have each participant choose one, then take a seat in a circle. Now, each woman in turn should give the name tag to its owner. Trying to remember the goals and owners will probably cause much laughter. But, it's also a good way to help participants think more about their goals. Ask the group to help anyone who isn't sure whose name tag she has. Ask everyone to wear her name tag.

2. Explain that this meeting will help the participants reach their goals. Tell them that we need **personal resources** and **community resources** in order to be successful.

3. Ask the participants to think about personal resrouces first. Have them think about their goal. What good qualities do they have that could help them reach their goals? For instance, one woman who wants to raise livestock may say she likes animals. Another woman may say she's very hardworking.

4. Go around the circle and ask each woman to name one good quality about herself that could help in reaching her goal. When all have finished, ask how they felt about naming good qualities. Point out that everyone has certain strengths. We need to know these strengths and appreciate them. They can help in reaching our goals.

5. Now, explain that community resources can also be important to us. Read the "Using Community Resources" story, using the flannelboard and figures to show the people in the story and their community. Write down the resources the participants suggest to aid the woman in the story.

6. To further help the women in reaching their own goals, ask them to identify:
   - What community resources can help you meet your own goal?

   Encourage them to give ideas to one another.

Ideas to take home
By the end of the activity, participants should know some specific personal resources and community resources to help them reach their goals.
   Take a short break.

Resources and planning for reaching our goals 4

Planning to reach a personal goal
(1 hour)

Purpose
Participants have now defined a personal goal, and the personal and community resources needed to reach it. In this activity, they will plan how they will achieve the goal.

Materials
Paper and pencil for each participant

Steps

1. To help participants understand the idea of a *plan of action,* begin by discussing something they've planned and done in their own lives. For example: planting crops, building a house, making a dress, planning a wedding, and so on.

2. After discussing a few things participants have planned and done, introduce the "five friends" for planning. Hold up your hand and for each finger, list one of the "friends":
   Why? The reasons for working toward a goal (motivation)
   Who? The person (people) who will carry out the plan
   How? The specific steps or tasks required
   When? The time each step will be done and the goal achieved
   What? The personal and community resources needed

3. Play a "memory game" so that participants learn the "five friends." Ask all the participants to stand and raise one of their hands in front of them. Go around the circle and have each participant name the "five friends" on her fingers. Anyone who succeeds can sit down; anyone who doesn't must try again the next time around. Keep going around the circle until each participant has listed the "five friends" correctly.

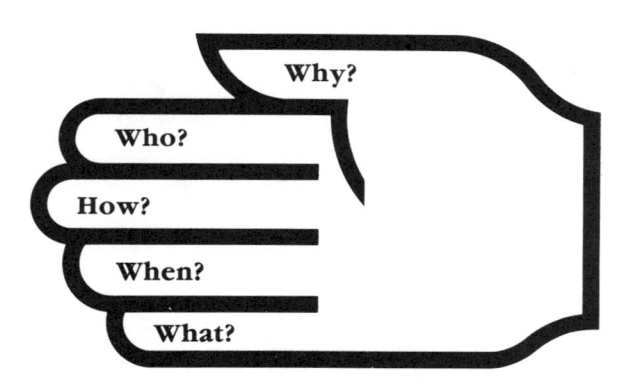

4. Knowing the "five friends," the participants are ready to make their own plans. Divide the participants into groups of three members. Give each participant paper and pencil. Ask them to trace their hands on the paper. In the small groups, each participant should discuss a plan using the fingers on the hand she drew. The two other members of the group should help make the plan. Literate groups can write their plans next to the fingers.

5. Bring the small groups back to the circle. Ask the participants if they had any difficulty in making their plans. Encourage them to talk about difficulties. Explain that it's natural to have some trouble at first.

6. Ask the participants to present their plans one by one to the group.

Ideas to take home
Make sure everyone ends the meeting with a clear plan. Compliment the women on their good work!

Materials 4

Using a flannelboard

A flannelboard is easy to make, easy to use, and portable. It can be used to illustrate stories, or to display audio-visual aids.

To make a flannelboard, you will need a rectangular piece of wood, fiberboard, or heavy cardboard. A board about 60 cm. x 45 cm. (2 ft. x 18 in.) is a good size. The board can be larger, as long as it is easy to carry.

Next, stretch a piece of flannel over the board and tack or tape it to the back of the board. Or, hem the flannel with elastic and slip the flannel piece over the board.

Figures for the flannelboard can be drawn or cut out of magazines. Glue the pictures to thin cardboard. Then, glue a piece of sandpaper, "velcro," or rough fabric to the back of the pictures so they will stick to the flannelboard.

To use the flannelboard, lean the board at a slight angle on a table, a chair, or any kind of stand. Pictures or figures placed on the flannelbaord can help tell a story. Drawings or charts can be used to show a problem situation or to provide information.

Encourage group members to place or move the pictures on the board themselves. This enables them to contribute actively to a meeting.

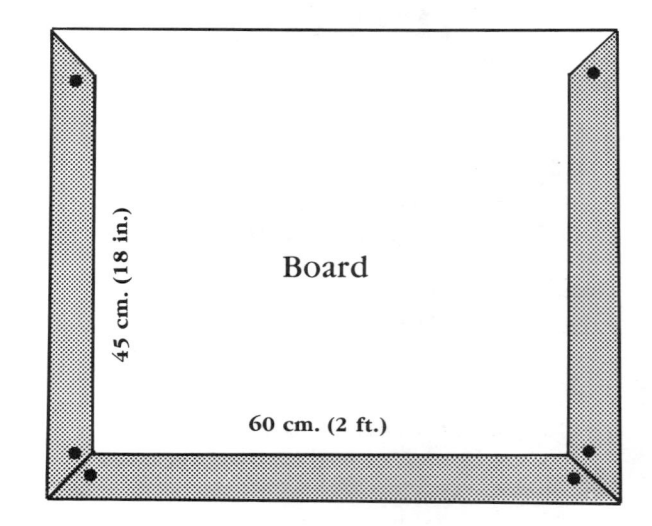

Flannel—

(fold at the edges and tack to the back of the board)

43

44

Community resources story
(use with flannelboard and figures)

(Name) has four children. She recently completed a course in repairing motorcycles. She would like to earn more money for her family and herself. Yesterday, (Name)'s cousin asked her to work during the afternoons at his garage. She's very excited by the offer. But, she worries about her children. They are still small, and there is no one at home to care for them during the day.

(Name) has set a goal. She wants to find a way that her children can be cared for so she can work. If (Name) lived in your community, what community resources could help her reach her goal?

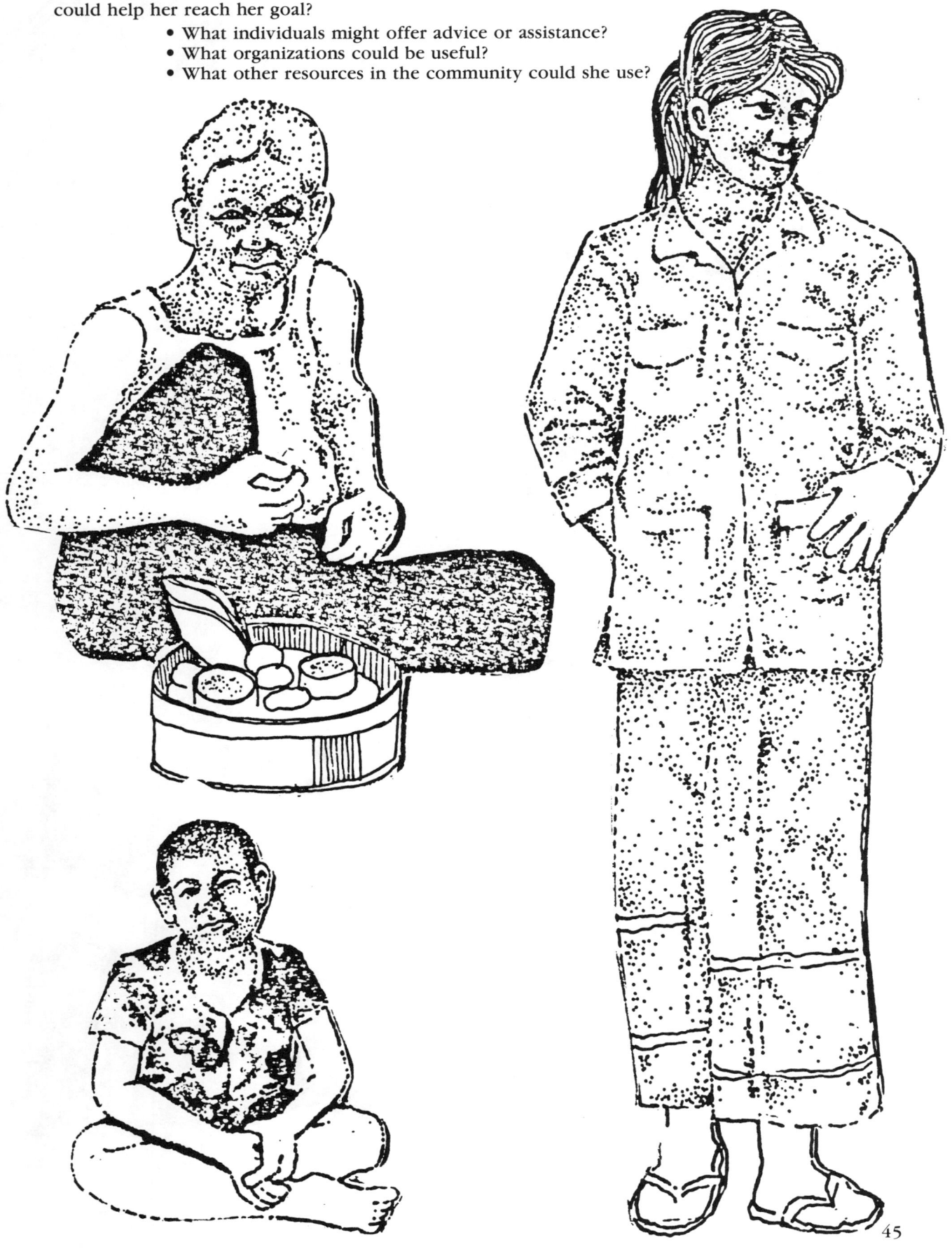

- What individuals might offer advice or assistance?
- What organizations could be useful?
- What other resources in the community could she use?

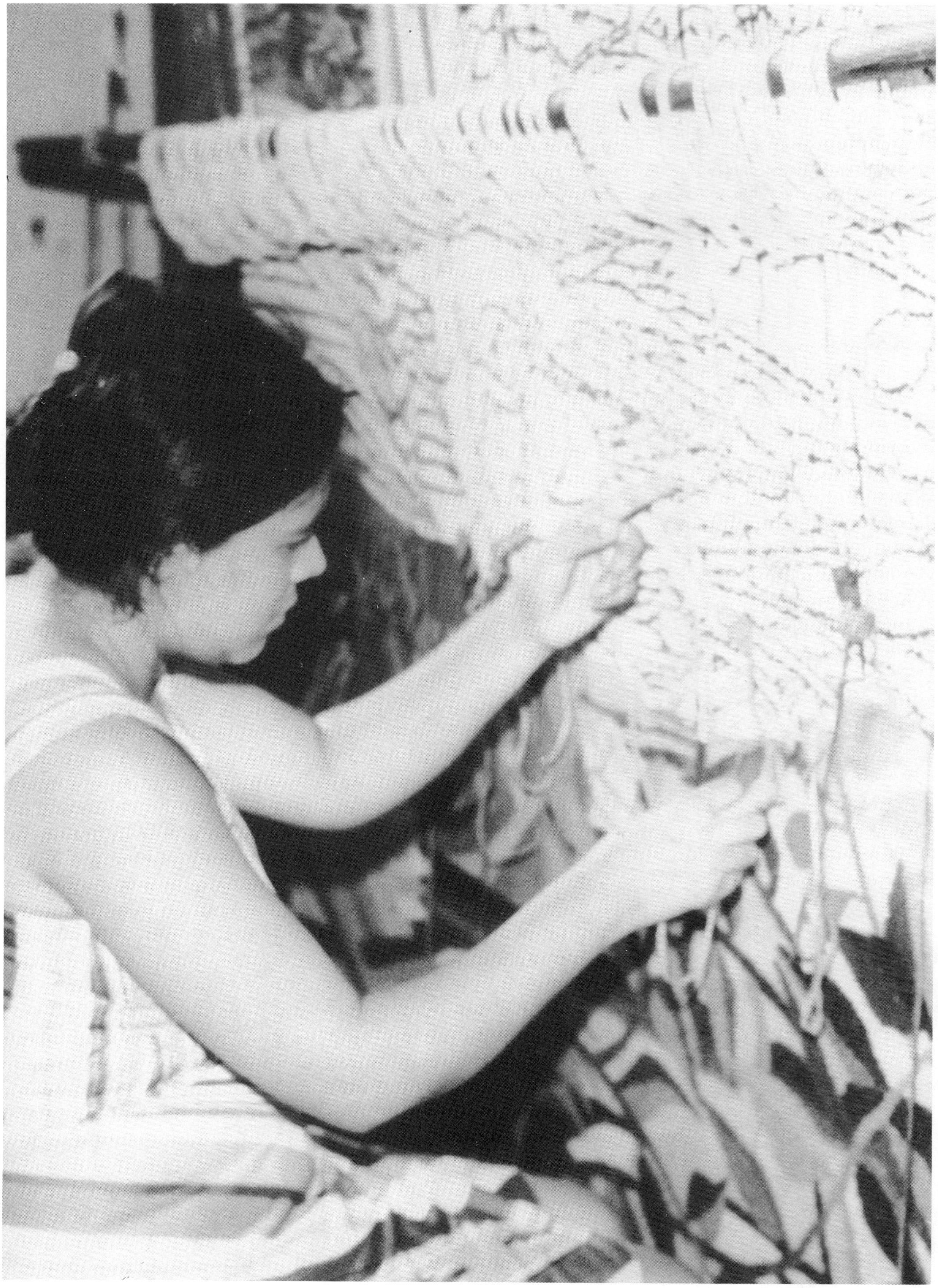

Women and work

Whether from urban barrios or rural villages, women often share a priority concern for how they can increase their family incomes. The four meetings that follow provide a way for women to identify and pursue profitable income-generating activities in their own locale.

Meeting 5 involves women in thinking about the kind of work women can do and the work options they'd like to explore. Meeting 6 takes the women outside the group meeting place, to visit resource people, employers, or training programs related to the work options that interest them.

In meeting 7, the women take a hard look at the profitability of different work options. They conduct their own market analysis. Finally, in meeting 8, the women use a simple action planning method to guide them in: improving or learning certain technical skills; starting a small business; or finding a job.

NOTE: For more extensive business training, see OEF's series "Appropriate Business Skills for Third World Women" (p. 104).

Ways to earn (1 hour)

Purpose
Many women have a narrow idea of the ways they can earn money. This thinking may keep them away from work that could enable them to increase their incomes. In the first activity, participants will discuss many kinds of jobs and ways to earn. In the second activity, they will decide on a few ways that most interest them. In Meeting 6, they then will find out about these work areas.

Materials
Newsprint and felt tip pens (or blackboard and chalk)
Note: Here is a useful booklet on ways for women to earn:
- "Women Making Money" (Newsletter #18): Available from International Women's Tribune Centre, 777 UN Plaza, New York, New York, 10017, U.S.A. (free).

Steps

1. Tell participants that this meeting is about the kinds of work they already do to earn money and the kinds of work they would like to do.

2. Divide the group into teams of four or five members. Have each team go to a different corner of the room and then explain what to do. They will plan the "Guess What Job" game, a game that uses acting but no words. Tell each team it should think of as many ways to earn money as possible. Examples might include: nursing, teaching, being a lawyer, sewing, working for the government, clerical work, pig-raising, rice or vegetable farming, electrical repair work, auto repair, factory work, and so on. Explain that members of each team will act out activities for other teams to guess. Help teams by acting out one way to earn money yourself.

3. Bring the teams back together. Explain that a member of the first team will act out a way to earn money. Then, a member of the second team acts, and so on, until all the teams have acted once.

4. Begin the game. Have the first team act out one way to earn money. The team that guesses correctly what work the first team is acting out receives a point (members of a player's own team cannot guess!). Each time a kind of work is guessed, put it on newsprint using stick figures or words.

5. After all teams have acted once, start with the first team again and continue until all teams can think of no more kinds of work. Important: Once a team has shown a way to earn, it cannot be done again by another team. No repeats!! At the end of the game, the team with the most points for guessing correctly is the 'winner'. If the list is short, add your own ideas for kinds of work.

6. Compliment the women on all their good ideas about kinds of work.

7. Next, begin to talk about work women do. What work can the women themselves do to earn more money?

   These questions can guide your discussion:
   - Which work on the list can be done by women? (Discuss each item on the list one by one.)
   - For work participants say cannot be done by women, ask "Why not? Are these reasons true?"
   - Which ways of earning money interest you the most? (Participants may be interested in improving their present work or in starting new work.)
   - What are the advantages and disadvantages of these options?

Ideas to take home
At the end of this activity, the women should have an idea of different work options—and the advantages and disadvantages of these options. In the next part of the meeting, they decide which options to explore more.

Take a five minute break.

Exploring different kinds of work

5

Women's work (1 hour)

Purpose
In this activity, participants choose a few possibilities for increasing their incomes. For Meeting 6, you will arrange for the women to meet a "resource person" to help them learn more about one or more of their choices.

Materials
Two simple—and funny—hand puppets/Make your own using "stick puppet" samples on pages 51-53 (or make puppets from small paper bags, socks, or other materials you have available)

Puppet skit/See instructions on page 52

Steps

1. This activity begins with a puppet skit. You can perform the skit with another facilitator or one of the participants. It is best to prepare the skit before the meeting. The instructions on page 50 will help you make your skit.

2. During the break, set up a puppet stage. This can be a table turned on its side, a cardboard box, or whatever is available.

3. To start, ask the women to sit in front of the stage. Tell them you'd like them to listen to (first puppet's name) and (second puppet's name). They will talk about how women earn money.

4. Perform the skit.

5. Then, begin discussion:
    - What did you think of the skit?
    - What did you think of the first puppet's ideas? the second puppet's ideas?
    - What did you agree with? What did you disagree with?
    - What did you think of the ideas about work women can do and can't do?

6. Participants have talked about different ways to earn money. Now, they can choose a few ways that they themselves want to pursue. To help them decide, ask:
    - What way or ways of earning would the group members like to know more about for themselves? (Make sure they consider whether they would like to: improve the work they already do; start a production group or small business; or find a job.) • Do these seem to be skills or products for which there is a real need?

7. Guide the women in thinking about different choices. Make sure they think about whether the choices of ways to earn are in demand. They will talk more about this in the next two meetings.

Ideas to take home
End the meeting when the women have agreed on the ways to earn that most interest them. Explain that the next meeting will enable them to find out more about these ways. Tell them that they will talk with a resource person or persons. If you plan a field trip (see "Preparation for Meeting 6"), discuss the arrangements for getting there. Make sure everyone knows where to meet and when, or how you will contact them to let them know. Ask participants for suggestions for people to meet. Also, ask for volunteers to help in contacting the resource persons.

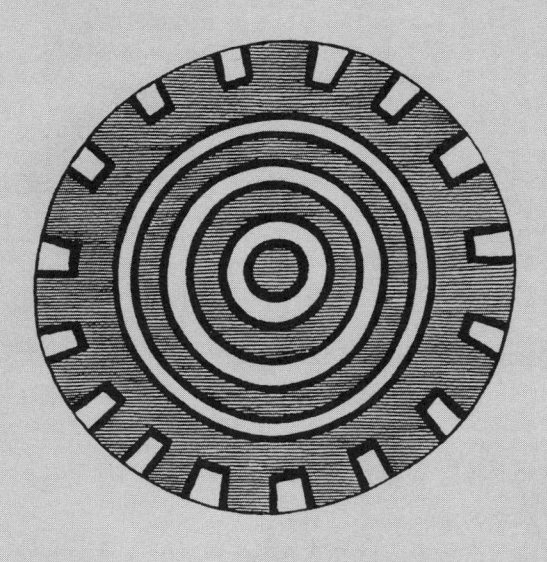

Preparation for Meeting 6

For the next meeting, you will need one or more resource people. You can arrange a "field trip" to visit a resource person at work, or you can invite the person to the group's meeting place. The "field trip" is best. The participants can see for themselves what a certain kind of work is like.

Who are resource people? Resource people need to know something about the ways to earn that interest the women. They can be government officials or professionals in agriculture, health, community development or other areas. They can be local people, like a woman who makes and sells soap, a man who raises big, healthy sheep, or a family that owns and operates a store. They can be potential employers, such as a factory, hotel, or store manager.

For instance, if your group wants to grow better crops, you might contact an extension agent. Or, if they want to repair small appliances, contact someone from a vocational training center or someone in the community who is good at fixing things. Or, you might contact someone who has a small business or belongs to a cooperative.

Remember: resource people do not have to have titles or be experts. They can be anyone who has the skills, information, or ideas that the participants need.

What should a resource person do? It's a good idea for you and some participants to meet with a resource person before the meeting. This helps the resource person know what the group needs.

A good resource person usually does three things: **show, tell,** and **answer.** To prepare the resource person for the meeting:
- Explain that the group would like to see the person at work, hear about what the work is like, and have some questions answered.
- Give the resource person background about the program and the participants.
- Offer to help the resource person prepare any materials for the presentation
- Encourage the resource person to be practical and to use demonstrations if possible.

The number of resource people you contact depends on the interests of the participants and how much time they have. The information in this box can help make your visits worthwhile!

Materials 5

"Women's work" puppet skit instructions

This is a skit or play about work opportunities for women in your community. Every community is different. So, your skit will be different than a skit done somewhere else.

Here are some guidelines for creating your skit:

1 Prepare the skit before the meeting. In the skit, you can talk without a script like you would in a conversation. Or, you can write down the words and read them. The skit should be about 10 minutes long.

2 Include at least two puppets in the skit. The puppets can be two women or a man and a woman. Give the puppets local names. You will take the part of one puppet. Another facilitator or participant takes the other puppet.

3 The first puppet thinks that women are good at cooking, sewing, and caring for children. If women work, they should only work as teachers, seamstresses, or in other similar jobs.

4 The second puppet thinks that women's income is important, even essential, to their families. This puppet thinks women can do many things. Women should try new kinds of work. They should try to find work that is interesting and profitable.

5 In the skit, the first puppet meets the second puppet. They have tea or some refreshment, then start talking. They talk about what kinds of work their daughters can do when they get older. They argue about kinds of work women can do and can't do.

Some ideas for kinds of work

Have the skit include ideas for wage employment (a job with a salary) and self-employment (an individual or group business). Include some ways to earn that people think of as "men's work," such as carpentry, electrical repair, or being a doctor.

6 Make the skit funny! The puppets can get very angry!!

7 **Remember:** Try to talk about kinds of work the women may not have considered. Help them think about new ideas. And also remember—to have fun!

53

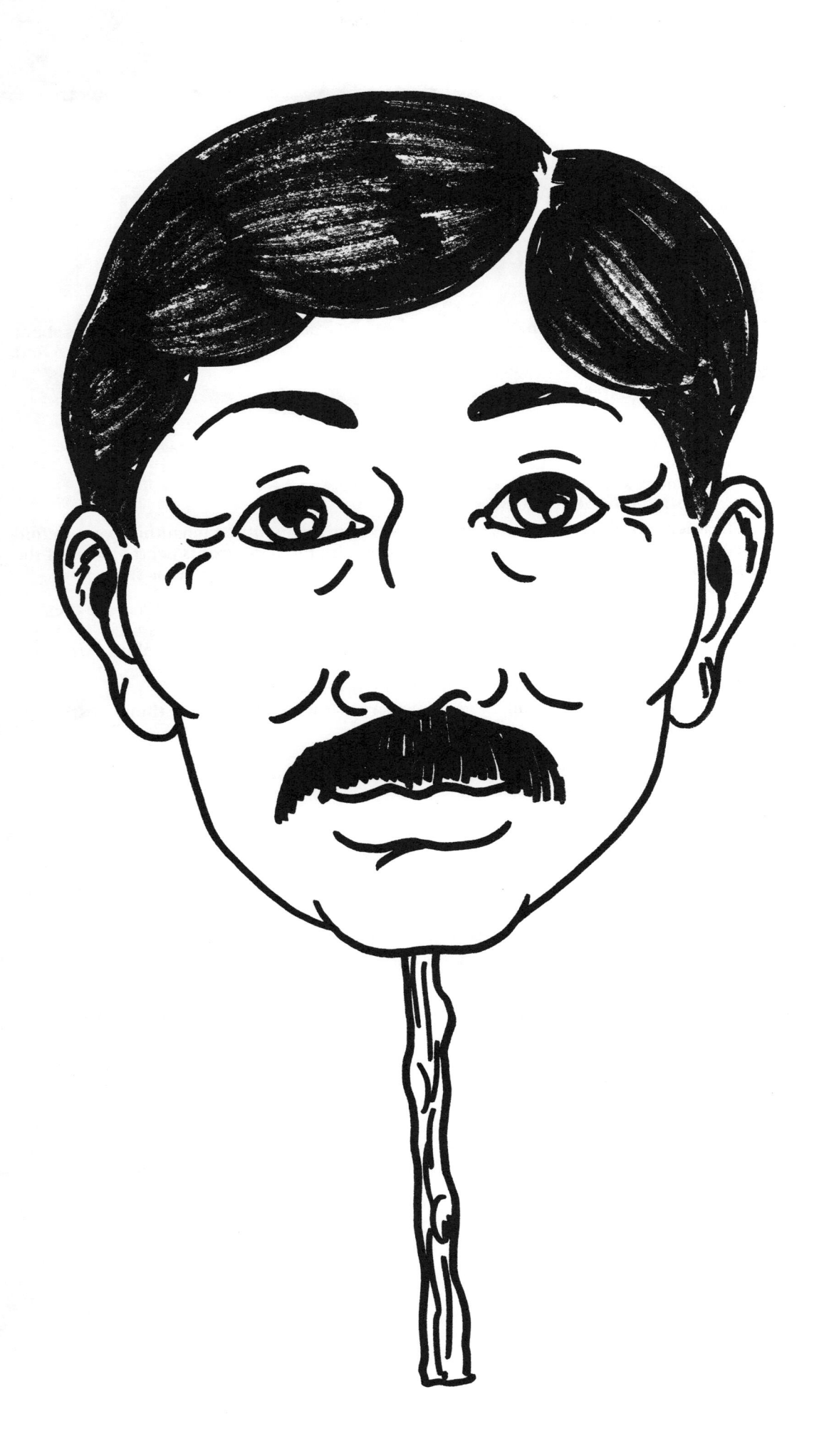

Contacting local resources

A visit with a resource person
(2 hours)

Purpose
Women meet with a resource person in this meeting. The resource person is someone who knows about one of the ways to earn chosen in Meeting 5. The visit with this local "expert" enables women to find out more about the kinds of work that interest them.

Materials
"Field trip" or resource person presentation/See Preparation for Meeting 6 on page 50

Steps

1. Before the meeting with the resource person, talk with participants about what they want to find out. If you go to the resource person's workplace, meet with the participants before going. If the resource person comes to the participants' meeting place, get together before he or she arrives.

2. Guide the women in thinking of questions they would like to have answered. Encourage them to ask about: how a product is produced, what skills are needed, what equipment is used, earnings, what problems to expect, and so on. For instance, a group interested in making and selling rattan furniture might ask:
   - How did the resource person learn rattan work?
   - What materials and equipment are necessary? How much do these things cost?
   - What technical skills are needed?
   - How long does it take to make a chair, a stool, and so on?
   - What problems can happen?
   - What is the marketing situation?
   - What kind of profit can be made?
   - What advice could the resource person give to the women?

3. If time allows, divide the participants into groups of four or five members. Have them brainstorm (list without discussing) questions they would like to ask. Write down the questions if possible.

4. Now the women are ready to meet with the resource person.
   Encourage the "expert" to show what she or he does and to talk about it. Make sure to leave enough time for the women's own questions. They can ask the questions on their lists and other questions they think of.

5. At the end of the meeting, thank the resource person. If appropriate, present some small token of appreciation.

Ideas to take home
After finding out about a particular way to earn, the women may decide that this way is something they would like to do. If so, then go on to Meeting 7. Or, the women may be doubtful or interested in other ways to earn too. If so, plan visits with other resource persons and the participants before Meeting 7.

Work options: Which is best? 7

Can I make a profit doing this work? (1-2 hours)

Purpose
In Meetings 5 and 6, the women identified ways to earn that interest them. This is important. But, it does not mean that the work is profitable. In this meeting, the women will judge whether the kind of work they like is also the kind of work that will enable them to make money. This meeting will be most useful for women who want to start a small business. It may also help women who want to find a job.

Materials
"Can I Make a Profit Doing This Work?" form (if possible, provide a form for each participant)/Use form on pages 56-57

Information on local and national market demands (sometimes available from government offices) or a person who knows about market demands, if available

Steps

1. In this meeting, you will guide the participants in determining the profitability of the work that interests them. Written information on market demands or a resource person can be useful. However, if they are not available, you and the women can do all right on your own.

2. Start the meeting by talking about the kind of work chosen by the women in Meeting 6. Then explain that when we want to choose a kind of work that will enable us to make money, we need to think of two things:
   - Am I interested in this kind of work?
   - Will I be able to make a profit from my work?

3. Tell the participants that this meeting will help them answer the second question.

4. Now, ask the women to close their eyes. Tell them to imagine themselves doing the kind of work they want to do. Ask them to make a picture in their minds of: working at a certain place; producing and selling a certain product; or providing a certain service.

5. Have participants open their eyes after a few minutes. Ask them to think of what they need to know to judge whether the work that interests them will be profitable. What questions can they think of?

6. Brainstorm (list without discussing) questions for 10 or 15 minutes. For instance, a group interested in producing rattan furniture might examine:
   - Where can we buy our supplies and materials?
   - How can we gain some new skills for using certain tools?
   - Why will people buy from us, rather than from other producers?
   - Where can we produce our products?
   - Where will we sell our products? How will we get our things to the marketplace?
   - Should we produce lampshades, chairs, and other things? Or, should we only make one thing?
   - How much can we produce in six months?
   - How much will we be able to earn?

7. When the group has listed many questions, given everyone a copy of the "Can I Make a Profit Doing This Work?" form. Have anyone who can read make sure the group's questions are all included on the form. Add those that aren't.

8. Divide the women into groups of five or six members. Each group should use the form to think about the kind of work they want to do. The groups should calculate the estimated profit of the work. With preliterate groups, you may decide not to divide into smaller groups. Their discussion can use the symbols on the form as a guide. Take about 20 or 30 minutes for completing the form.

9. Bring the small groups back together. Ask each group to report on its profit estimation.

10 Finally, ask the group to answer this question:
- Is the work we've been discussing likely to be profitable and worth doing?

Ideas to take home

This meeting ends with the women being more sure of the work they want to do, or having doubts about it. If they are quite sure of what they want to do, go on to Meeting 8. If they have doubts, it will be helpful if you can find out information to help answer their questions. Contact another resource person or hold another discussion meeting. When participants are finally more sure of what work to pursue, then begin Meeting 8.

"Can I make a profit doing this work?"

This form will help you find out the "profit" that you can make from a certain kind of work. It is important to know the estimated profit in order to decide if a certain work or job is worth doing. You may also have other reasons for doing or not doing a certain kind of work.

Expenses: 6 months _____ 1 year _____

Look at the boxes below. Use the categories and questions to discuss the work you want to do. What are some of the costs you will have? For instance, for a job, you may have training and transportation expenses. For a small business, you may have expenses in all the categories.

Estimate how much your business or job will cost in six months and one year. Write these estimates in the blanks above.

Skills	What skills are needed? How do I get these skills: from people? from training programs? How long will it take to learn these skills? How much will training cost?
Equipment Facilities	What is needed: equipment; supplies; a place to work; a place for storage? Where can I get these things? How much will they cost?
Capital	Is any "start-up" money needed? How much? Where can I get this money? Do I need credit? from where? How much will the interest be?
Transportation	What will be needed: personal travel; transportation of goods? What transportation is available? How much will it cost?
Promotion	What kind of advertising will I use? How much of my time will this take? How much will it cost?
Personnel	What kind of organization will I have? Who will I work with? Who will manage? keep the accounts? How much will I need to pay these people?

Materials 7

Problems ❓	What problems can I expect? How can I avoid these problems? How much could these problems cost?

Income: 6 months_____ 1 year_____

Look at the boxes below. Use the upper box if you are starting a small business.
Use the lower box for a job.
Use the questions to estimate how much you will earn in six months and one year.
Write the estimates in the blanks above.

Sales	How much will I produce? What will be the selling price? Is there a need for my product or service? Who will buy what I have to sell? Why will they buy it? How often? Who else is selling the same thing? How much can I sell in six months? a year? How much will I earn from sales?
Salary	How much will I earn in wages in six months? a year?

Profit:

Income: 6 months _____ 1 year _____

− Expenses: 6 months _____ 1 year _____

= Profit: 6 months _____ 1 year _____

Write your expense and income estimates in the blanks above. Subtract expenses from income.
Now you know your estimated profit.

Is this work profitable and worth doing?

Use your estimated profit to decide if you want to start a certain business or get a certain job.
- Will your profits be more than your present profits?
- What are the advantages and disadvantages of the work?
- Is this the work you want to pursue?

Making a plan of action

Better together than alone (45 minutes)

Purpose
In previous meetings, participants decided the work they want to pursue. This meeting enables them to make a plan of action for doing so. In the first activity, they think about how they want to work: alone or together?

This activity is designed for women who want to start a small business. For women who want to find a job, skip this activity and do the next, "Planning a Way to Earn More."

Materials
"Better Together Than Alone" Script/Use script on pages 60-61

Three "actors" who can read (three participants; yourself and two participants; or yourself and two friends)

Steps

1. Begin the meeting with the skit. If possible, have the "actors" practice the skit once or twice before it's presented.

2. After the skit, ask these questions:
   - What did everyone think of the skit?
   - Who agreed with Poncha? Why?
   - Who agreed with Prisca? Why?
   - The group has thought about certain kinds of work. What are the advantages to forming a joint enterprise, such as a cooperative? What are the disadvantages?

3. Encourage the women to express their opinions on working together and working alone. Take about 15 or 20 minutes for this discussion.

4. Ask the group to decide amongst themselves whether the whole group or smaller groups want to plan to work together.

Ideas to take home
End the activity when the participants have made some decision about whether or not they want to work together.

Take a five minute break.

Planning a way to earn more (1¼ hours)

Purpose
This activity helps participants decide what steps they need to take in order to try to earn more money. Women may want to plan how to: improve or learn technical skills; start a small business; or find a job.

Materials
Sample "Planning Chart"/Make your own using sample on page 61

Large pieces of paper or cardboard, at least 60 cm. x 90 cm. (2 ft. x 3 ft.) (one for each small group); colored paper and felt tip pens; scissors; glue (or, four charts already prepared)

Steps

1. Explain to participants that they will now plan what they need to do to earn more money. Begin by asking, "What is planning?" For groups who completed Meeting 4, remind them about the plans they made to reach their personal goals. For other groups, ask them to think about plans they make in their own lives for: planting crops, building a house, making a dress, and so on.

2. Divide into groups of four or five members. If the entire group decides it wants to work cooperatively, members will have a chance to get together at the end of the meeting. If only some participants decide to work as a cooperative, make sure they are in the same group. See the box below for some ideas about what groups should discuss in making their plans.

> ### Things to think about for planning ways to earn
> In Thailand, the village women decided to start their own small businesses to produce and sell chickens, fish, cloth, and other products.
>
> The Thai groups encountered many issues that other groups may need to think about too.
>
> Here are some of these issues: marketing the products; access to resources; availability of credit; how to set up and manage a small enterprise; learning needed skills; and how to work as a cooperative.

3. Show your sample planning chart. Ask each group to make a chart. In each pocket, they will put a "task card" for a step they need to take. Help them identify some steps for the kind of work they are planning to do. For instance, for making rattan furniture, the first step might be to make arrangements with a local artisan to give lessons in rattan weaving. The next step might be to purchase a small quantity of supplies. And so on. Make sure the participants include dates for completing the tasks!

4. Give the small groups about 30-40 minutes to make their charts and their action plans.

5. While the groups are making their plans, visit each one to answer questions or give suggestions.

6. Have each team present its chart. If the whole group is planning to work together on an income generation activity, combine all the tasks onto one chart.

Ideas to take home

This meeting ends the four meetings on "women and work." The women in your program now probably have a better idea of opportunities for earning and how to use these opportunities. The door is open. But, some will still take time to walk through it. Or, those who do may find obstacles on the other side, such as lack of child care facilities. Your support, or the support of other resource people, is very important for helping the women follow through on their plans. They may need encouragement and advice.

Finding a job or starting a small business takes time. These meetings have been a first step. Women who plan a small business enterprise will probably need some technical assistance. Use the materials listed on pages 47 and 48 or find local people who know about business management and accounting. Also, use Meeting 11, "Ways to Borrow" (page 76) for women who need credit.

Materials

"Better together than alone" (script)

Introduction: Doña Poncha, Doña Prisca and Doña Chon are three women neighbors in Barrio Buena Vista. They are talking about the best way to solve their economic problems. Let's listen to them as they talk.

Poncha Sometime I'd really like to get together and chat.

Prisca Go ahead, then, speak! (Chon arrives)

Chon What are you two talking about so secretively?

Prisca Poncha says she wants to get together and discuss something.

Chon So what's it all about?

Poncha OK, this is the problem. I don't know about you two, but I think we should get together and think about what we can do to solve the terrible economic problems we are facing.

Chon Really, it's impossible to make it these days. All the prices have gone up and the money just doesn't stretch far enough any more.

Prisca Do you remember the discussion at our last few meetings? Some said women could do any kind of work.

Chon Sure—even go to the moon. What do you think?

Prisca I can just see myself driving one of those machines on my way to the stars! (They laugh)

Poncha It's nothing to laugh at Prisca, this is serious.

Chon You're right, Poncha.

Poncha OK, in our meetings, we've been talking about how we could make more money—we mentioned some jobs and professions, but we also talked about forming a cooperative.

Prisca I don't like the idea of cooperatives. I prefer to work alone.

Chon Things are bad. But why complicate my life?

Poncha And if Juan should die on you, then what?

Chon I can manage making and selling tortillas. (Note: Use a local food.)

Poncha But think how expensive it is to live! How are you going to feed and clothe and educate that brood of kids you have? You can't pay for that with egg shells. And what do you say, Prisca?

Prisca I'd like to open a business and sell clothes.

Poncha That's fine, but don't you think it would be better if we all put our efforts together in this business?

Prisca What?

Poncha What I'm trying to say is that we should unite and form a cooperative. One sunny day does not make a summer. (Note: This is a local expression in Honduras.)

Chon But I still think I'm better off alone. I don't want to get involved in problems of business or cooperatives.

Prisca Well, what I want is to make more money.

Poncha If we could join together to form a cooperative we'd not only be able to solve our family problems but also the problems of the community. We could have the day care center we need so badly, a clinic...

Chon It's true...and the kids need a playground. But still, we've always lived poor and not having all these things hasn't killed us yet.

Poncha Chon! What a conformist. We've got to find a way out of this misery. Look at how bad the streets are, we don't have

	running water or lights or garbage service. If we unite, we can solve these problems.
Chon	You're beginning to convince me, Poncha. I think you're right.
Prisca	Well, you still don't convince me.
Poncha	Alone, Prisca, you're not going to be able to accomplish very much.
Prisca	A lot of people have gotten rich working alone.
Chon	And stepping on simple people like you.

Poncha	Especially for us poor folks, Prisca, we really need to unite. Because it's the only way to honestly resolve our economic problems. Don't forget the saying: "In union there is strength."
Prisca	Well, you still don't convince me.

—This skit was created by Norma Marina Garcia, Hortensia Fonseca Espinal, and Edith Falck in Honduras.

Sample planning chart

Making a planning chart

To make a flexible planning chart you will need a large piece of cardboard or poster board and several heavy strips of paper as wide as the large board. Glue the bottoms and ends of the strips to the board. Folded slips of paper containing "tasks" can then be inserted into the "pocket" made by the strips.

Adapted from: *The Impertinent PERT chart* by Lyra Srinavasan, (New York: World Education, January 1977).

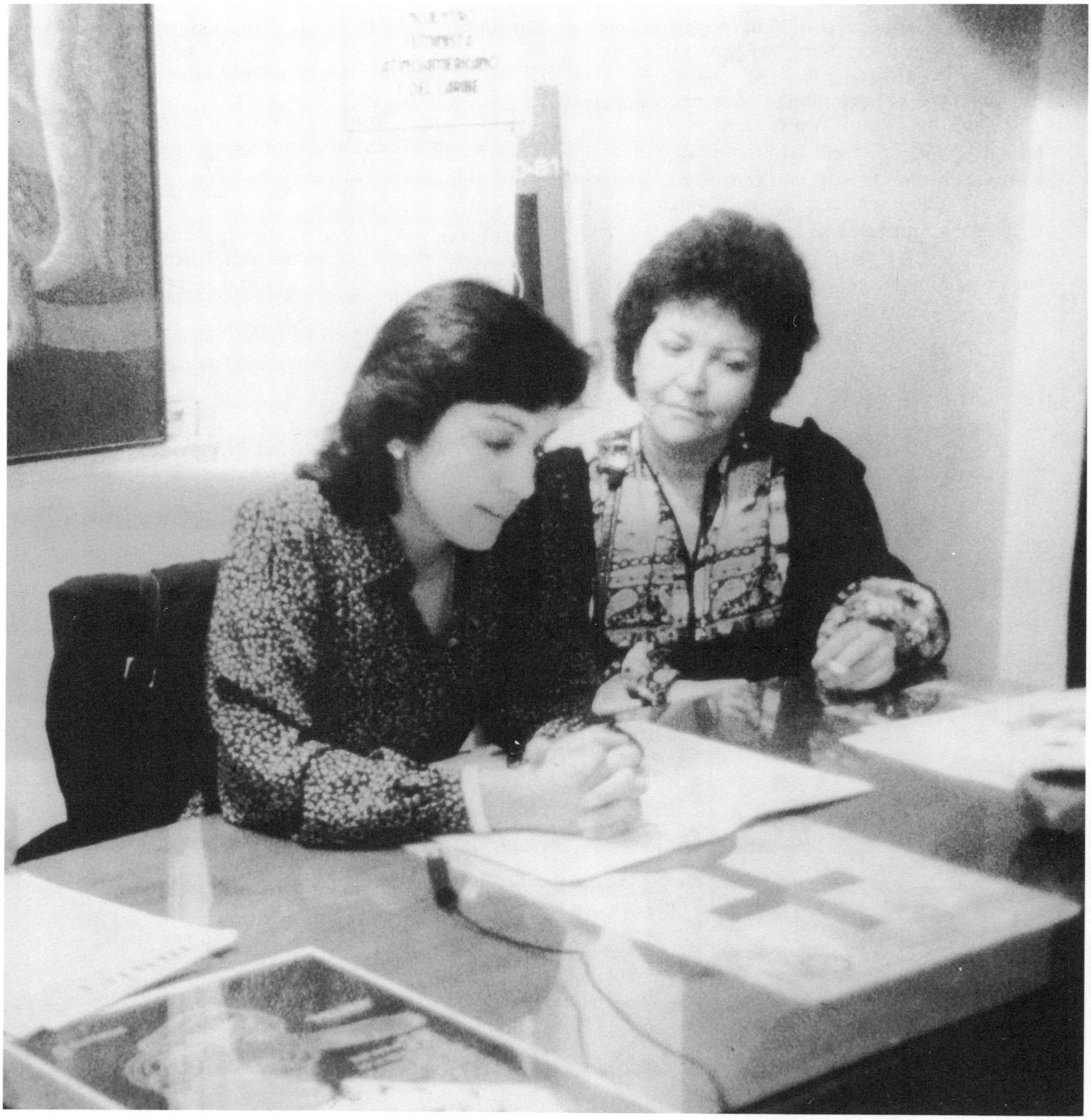

Working together

A group has more resources for solving a problem and usually has more power than a person acting on her own. Many of the problems women face can best be solved through group effort.

In Meeting 9, women consider the advantages of working as a group. Then, they develop their own guidelines for cooperating and making decisions together.

All the skills for working as a group cannot be gained in one meeting. These skills are developed over time, through involvement in group efforts. Other meetings in the handbook provide more opportunities for working as a group.

Building group strength

Advantages of groups (45 minutes)

Purpose
The first part of this meeting shows the advantages of cooperative group action over individual action. The activity helps participants think about the value of working as a group. A group can often accomplish a task more quickly and effectively than an individual can.

Materials
A bag containing about 20 local objects (such as articles of clothing, utensils, thread, a stone, and so on)

Two posters: A woman visiting an office alone and women visiting an office together/Make your own using posters in photos on page 67

Steps

1. Begin by saying that you'd like everyone to play a "memory game." Don't tell participants the purpose of the game. Dump all the objects from the bag onto a table. Tell participants that everyone should try to remember all the objects as you put them back in the bag. Put these objects in the bag one at a time. When you put each object in the bag, say what it is. Give participants a chance to look at it. But, don't go too slowly.

2. When all the objects are in the bag, explain that one individual alone will try to remember the objects and the other group members together will try to remember the objects. Explain that this is not a competition. But, it will be interesting to compare the results of individual effort and group effort. Ask for one volunteer who will try to remember the objects on her own.

3. Meet with the volunteer and write down her list. Then, meet with the other group members and write down their list. The volunteer and the group should be far enough apart so they cannot hear each other. For literate groups, write the lists on newsprint so they can be compared.

4. Bring the individual back to the group. Read her list first. For literate groups, post the newsprint. For pre-literate groups, take the objects from the bag as you read the list. Then, read the group list. Make sure to compliment the volunteer for her contribution. In almost all cases, groups will do better than individuals on this task. So she shouldn't feel like she's failed.

5. Discuss the results of the "memory game." The difference between the two lists should be clear, unless the volunteer had a very, very good memory. Encourage the participants to think about why the group list was longer. What does this tell them about the strengths of groups?
   - Compare the two lists. Which is longer? (If the individual and group lists are almost the same, point out how unusual this is and how groups usually tend to remember more.)
   - Why was the group able to complete the task better than the individual? What strengths do groups have that individuals don't have?
   - Show the two posters. How would you compare the two pictures? Who do you think will be more effective? Why?
   - Think about your own life. What could you do better as a member of the group than as an individual?

6. If your group has completed the previous four meetings on "Women and Work," also ask:
   - What ideas did the game give us about cooperative work activities?

Ideas to take home
Summarize some of the advantages and strengths of "working as a group" which the participants identified. Note that groups can have disadvantages, too. Sometimes groups are ineffective because members do not know how to work together. However, group activity is important in all our lives. We can use it to accomplish goals and to solve problems. The next activity will help participants improve skills to be effective group members.

Take a short break.

Group decision-making and cooperation (1¼ hours)

Purpose
By the end of this activity, participants will have developed guidelines for working together effectively and productively. They can then use these guidelines for small group activities during and after the program.

Materials
Newsprint and felt tip pens

Two sets of materials for "Making Something" (Each set should include six bags containing the following objects: Bag #1—scissors; Bag #2—string and felt tip pens; Bag #3—glue; Bag #4—lots of colored paper; Bag #5—a magazine with many photos; and Bag #6—a large piece of cardboard (at least 60 cm. x 90 cm. [2 ft. x 3 ft.]; this will obviously not fit in a bag so can be attached to it)

Steps

1. In this activity, it's not so important what participants do but how they do it. The "Making Something" game involves the women in working together. They will discuss what the group members did well, the problems they experienced, and what they might be able to do better. Take care that the group members do not feel they did not do a good job on "Making Something." Stress that we all have a lot to learn about cooperating and making decisions together.

2. Tell participants that this session is about working together effectively as a small group. We can learn most about how groups work by actually doing a group activity and thinking about what happened. Emphasize that there are no "right" or "wrong" ways to carry out the task of "Making Something."

3. Divide the participants into four groups. Two groups should include six members each. The other two groups can include all the remaining participants. (With a smaller number of participants, have one group of six and another group of the remaining participants.)

4. Meet with the two groups of six members each. These two groups will do the "Making Something" game. Then meet with the other two groups. These groups will be the "observers." Make sure to meet with the observers separately from the groups "Making Something." These groups should not know what the observers are watching.

5 Here is what to explain to the two kinds of groups:

To the groups "Making Something":
—Each group will sit at opposite ends of the room.
—Each member will be given a bag containing one of the six materials from the "Making Something" set.
—The group will have 20 minutes to make something together. Members can make anything they like and work together any way they choose.
—Group members can talk to one another but not to the observers.

To the groups of "Observers":
—One group of observers will be matched with one group "Making Something."
—The groups "Making Something" have been told that they have 20 minutes to create something. They can make anything they like and work together any way they choose.
—You may not talk to the members who are "Making Something."
—Your job is to watch how the group works together. How do they decide what to do? How do they cooperate?

6 Seat the groups "Making Something" in their separate places. The observers should sit in a circle around them. Give each group member one of the six bags. Tell them to open their bags and to begin. Remind them that they have 20 minutes to make something together. Literate observers should take notes on what they see.

7 At the end of 20 minutes, stop the groups even if they are not finished. Have each group show the other what it's made or begun to make.

8 Then, bring all the participants back to the circle for a discussion. First, ask the following set of questions to the observers. Then, ask the same questions to participants. Compare the responses.

- What happened in the two groups? Were they able to complete their task?
- How did members of each team feel? Satisfied? Frustrated? Why?
- How did the group decide what to do? Who made the decision? How? Did the group have a leader or leaders?
- Were all the six materials used? Why or why not? Did all group members contribute their own resources and ideas?
- What difficulties did the group members have in working together? How could these difficulties be avoided?

9 Participants will be working together during the rest of the program. What guideline(s) can participants set: for reaching a group decision? for using resources? for cooperating? Record these ideas on newsprint, if possible. Add some of your own ideas too (see box for examples).

> **Group guidelines**
> One group of women had these ideas for working effectively as a group:
> 1. Give everyone a chance to talk. One person should not talk all the time.
> 2. Listen to the person talking. Respect everyone's ideas.
> 3. Try to reach decisions that everyone can agree on.
> 4. Decide clearly what action the group will take. Also, decide what each person will do.

10 From all the ideas suggested, have participants choose five "rules" about working together effectively in their income-generation activities and other group efforts. Make sure to write these down and save them!

Ideas to take home

This activity has a product: the "rules" participants themselves set for working together. Participants can use these rules in future meetings. This will help participants remember them and use them when they are in groups outside the program.

Review what the participants did during the activity. They looked at their own experience and set some guidelines for being effective in groups. Compliment them on their guidelines.

Materials 9

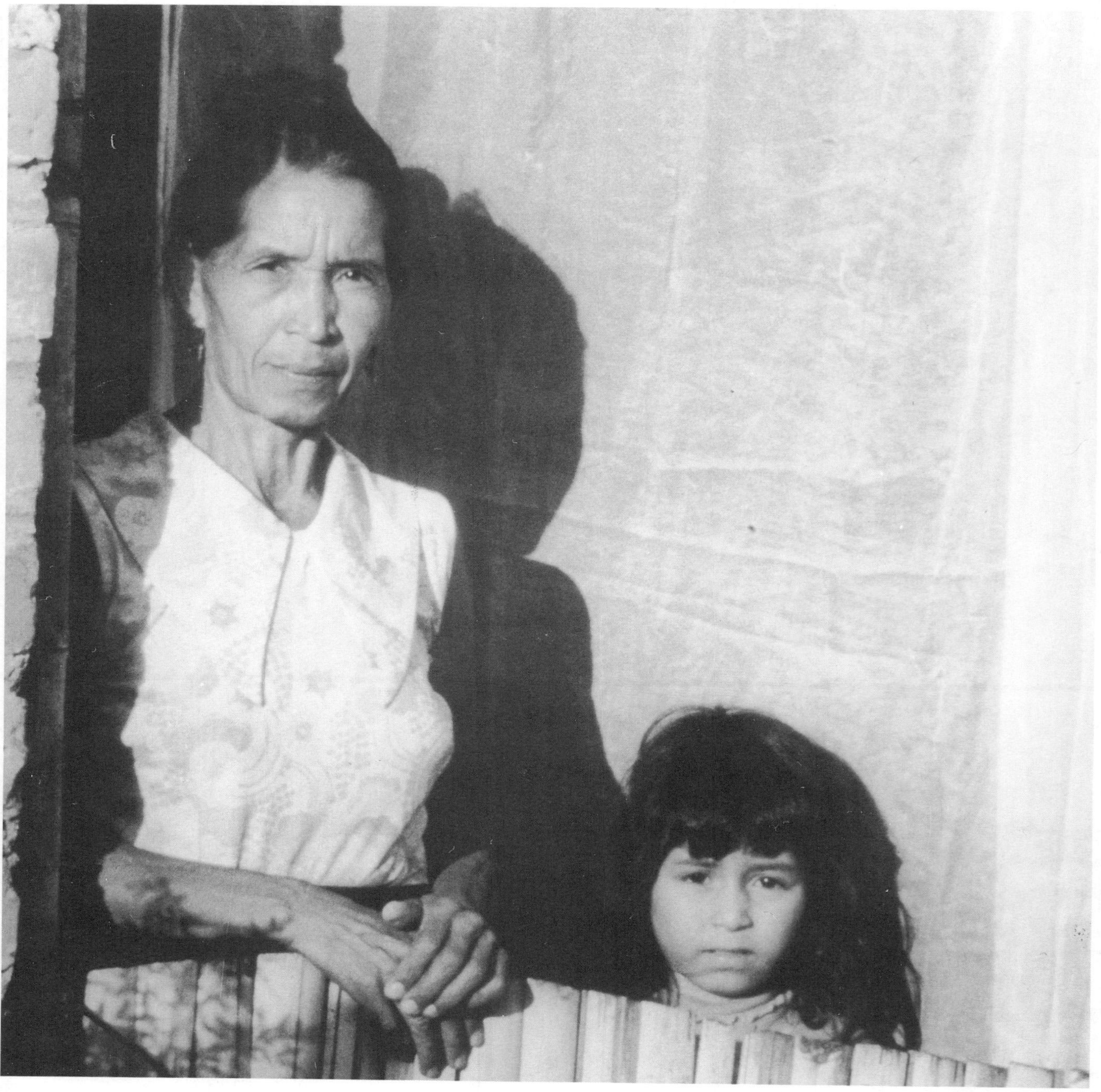

Women and their families

Family life is a vital concern to women. As mothers or daughters, wives or grandmothers or aunts, women experience many responsibilites and opportunities that profoundly affect their lives.

This section focuses on two parts of family life, relationships and finances. Meeting 10 gives women a chance to think about their household responsibilities and family members. In Meeting 11, the women identify ways to save and to borrow. They discuss possible sources of credit in their locale and how to tap these sources.

Family relationships

Sharing responsibility (1 hour)

Purpose

This activity will help participants think about how they use their time each day. They will identify ways they can make more time for things they want to do.

The women in your program are probably busy from morning til night. They must do many things to help themselves and their families to survive. Much of what they do has to be done. You can help participants to consider how they might "save time" by sharing tasks with family members. They will probably not be able to "save" a lot of time. But they will be able to save some—and that can make a difference.

Materials

Flannelboard and figures/See sample in Meeting 4 (pages 43-45)
Newsprint and felt tip pens
Two posters: Women doing tasks alone and family sharing tasks/Make your own using samples on pages 72-74

Steps

1 Explain that this activity will help participants to identify how to "find" time in their busy days to do some thing(s) they'd like to do.

2 Ask for a volunteer to describe what she did the previous day, from the time she got up til the time she went to bed. Ask her to use the flannelboard and figures to tell her story. Record each task or activity she mentions on newsprint (use stick figures or symbols for preliterate groups and words for literate groups).

3 Then ask the participants if their day was similar to hers. Have them name things they did that are not on the list. Add these suggestions. Put the list aside.

4 Now, ask participants to name things they like to do, but haven't had time. Record their responses on newsprint. Some examples might be: taking a child to see the doctor, visiting a friend, making a dress, seeing an extension agent, and so on.

5 When the second list is complete, post the first list next to it. Point out to participants that they may be able to do some of the things they'd like to do. Have they thought of sharing the tasks on the first list?

6 Show participants the two posters of a woman doing tasks alone and of a woman sharing tasks. Use these posters to start the discussion.

7 In the discussion, help participants to talk about sharing tasks and to identify which specific tasks could be shared and with whom. The participants may have strongly different opinions on the idea of sharing. Promote discussion among various participants rather than between the participants and yourself:

- How do you think the woman in the first picture feels? Do you ever feel this way?
- How does the woman in the second picture feel? What do you think of the picture? What are your reactions to what you see?
- Look at the first list of tasks you made. Which of those could you share with someone else? Why or why not?
- What could you ask your husband to do? Your children? Other people? What would be their reactions?

8 If there is time, have participants act out how to discuss sharing with their husbands, children, or other relatives.

Ideas to take home

Each participant should end the activity with an idea of what action she might take at home. But don't force everyone to do something. The idea of sharing may not be comfortable for all the women.

Take a five minute break.

10

Our husbands/companions, our children, our relatives (1 hour)

Purpose
This part of the meeting lets women discuss problems that family members may have. It also helps women build a support group for each other. Women themselves are often the best resources for knowing how to cope with different problems.

Materials
Paper and pens or pencils

Cassette tape recorder and tape, if available

Steps

1. Ask the participants if they has ever asked a friend for advice. Explain that in this activity, participants will give advice to one another. One group will write a "problem letter" to another group. That group will discuss how to solve the problem.

2. Divide participants into groups of five or six members. Your need an even number of groups for this activitiy. Now, ask each group separately to think about a problem that could occur with another family member: their husbands or companions, their children, or relatives. For ideas, tell them to think about their own experience or the experience of their friends. Explain that the letter should be written from one imaginary friend to another. Though the problem is imaginary, it is likely to be similar to the participants' own situations.

3. Have each group discuss different kinds of problems and then decide on one problem for the problem letter. Literate groups can write their own letters. With preliterate groups, you can write the letters for them or use the cassette tape. The letters should not be too long.

4. Ask each group to exchange its letter with one other group. These groups then read the letter (or have it read) and discuss what advice to give. Tell each group to discuss the causes of the problem and to identify alternative solutions before deciding on what advice to give.

5. Bring the entire group back together. Ask each group to describe the problem letter it received and the advice group members recommend. After each report, encourage other participants to suggest their ideas too. Discuss any important issues which arise. Or, ask participants if they have any other problems they would like to bring up.

Ideas to take home
At the end of this meeting, participants may have new ideas for dealing with specific concerns of their own family or friends. In the future, they may feel they can turn to other group members for support, if they need some encouragement or advice.

Materials 10

73

ATORN KHAMASIRI

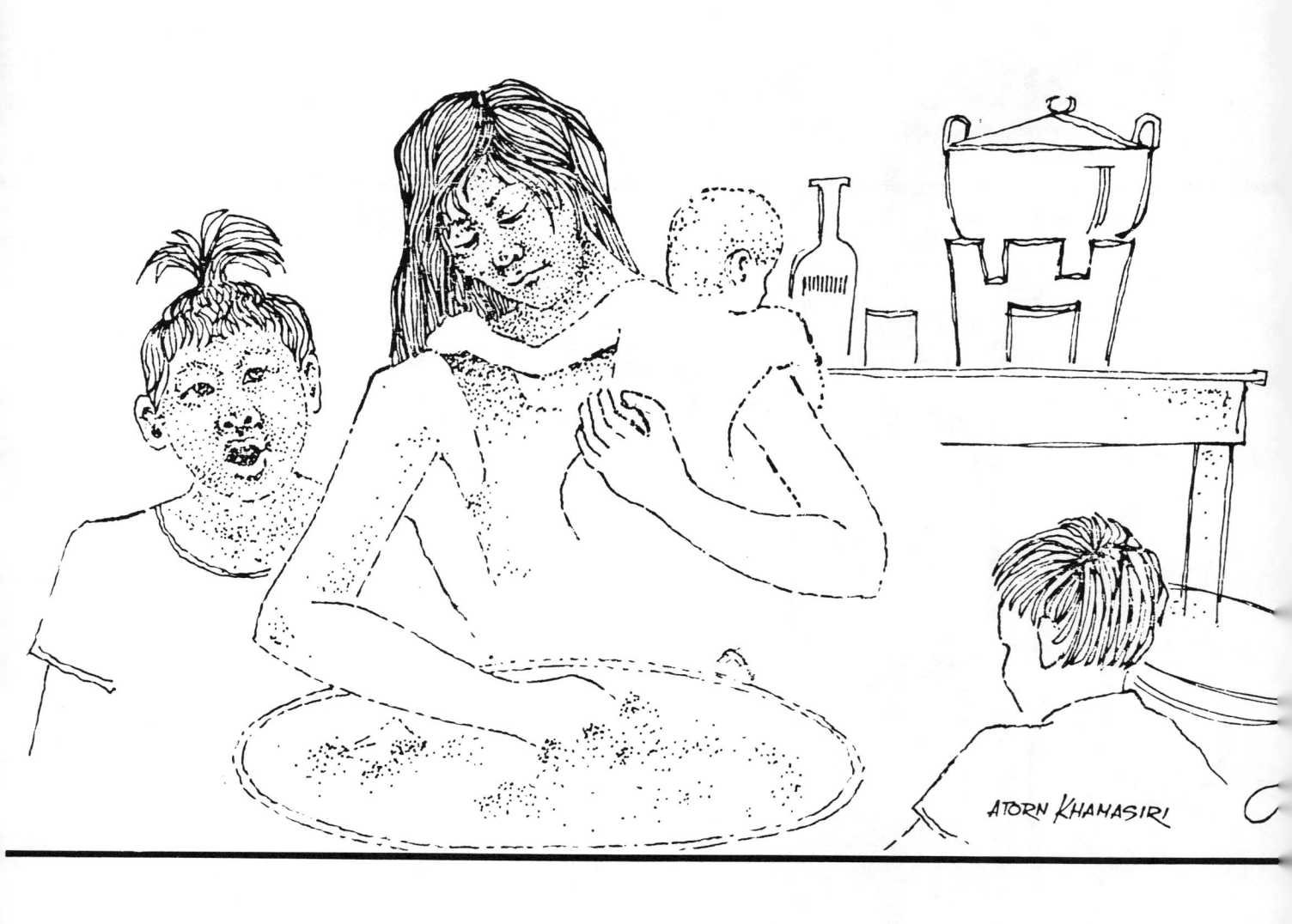

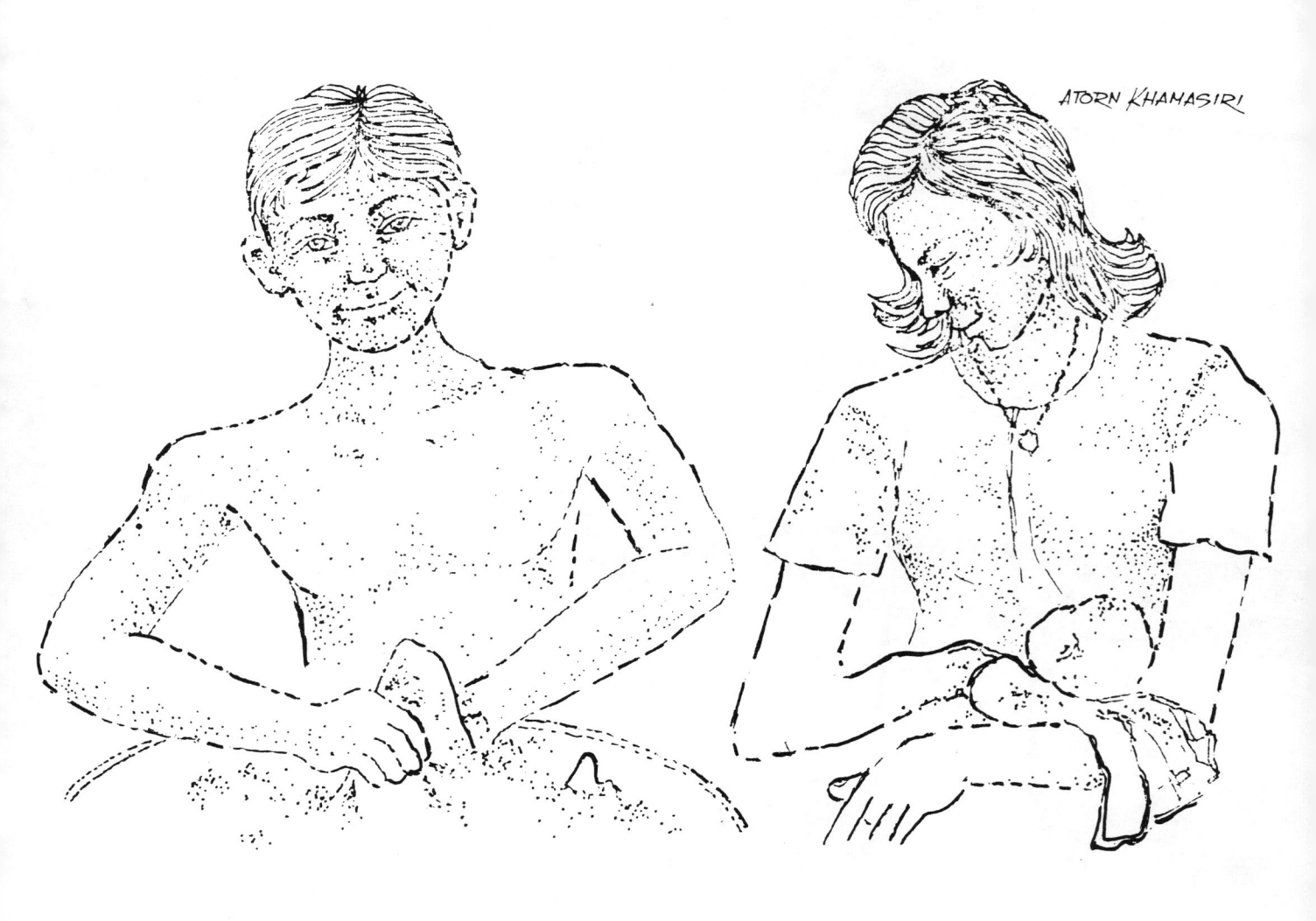

ATORN KHAMASIRI

Family finances 11

Ways to save (45 minutes)

Purpose
In this meeting, participants identify ways they can save money and borrow money. Before the activity, find out about banks and savings programs in your area.

Materials
Flannelboard and figures (symbols for "food," "housing," "clothing," and other things women spend money on each week; symbols for money, in small denominations)
Information on banks and savings programs

Steps

1   Explain to participants that this meeting is about family finances: how they spend money, how they might save, and how they might obtain credit.

2   Set up the flannelboard. Ask women what they spend money on each week. When they name an item, such as "food," put up the symbol on the board. After four or five items are listed, ask the women to decide approximately how much they spend each week for each item. Put the amounts next to the items they match.

3   Now, ask the participants to name other expenses that don't occur every week and that may be difficult to find money for. Some of these expenses may be: school supplies or uniforms, home repairs, medicine, fertilizer, trips, holiday celebrations, gifts, and so on. When a number of items have been given, ask how it's possible to pay for these things. Suggest that one way is "saving."

> ### How to start a Savings Club
> One way of savings has been used by women's groups in many settings: the savings club. Here's how it works. Each week, the women contribute a small amount to the savings "jar." Then, every two weeks or once a month (the time determined by the group members), one member in turn receives all the money to use as she pleases. This gives each group member a fairly large quantity of money at one time. This would not be possible if they saved only on their own. Women sometimes use this money for a major family expense or as "capital" for beginning a small business.

4   Ask the women for their ideas about how to save. Encourage them to talk about individual ways to save and group ways to save. Also, ask for ideas about what can help and hinder saving. Give any information on savings programs you have and any of your own ideas. The "savings club" is an idea you might want to suggest.

5   After a few ways to save are discussed, have the participants think about:
   - What are the advantages and disadvantages of the different ways to save?
   - What problems might happen when trying to save? How can these be avoided?
   - What way or ways would group members like to try?

Ideas to take home
For those interested in a savings program, help them decide what their next step will be. Do they need more information? Who should they contact? When will they begin?
   Take a five minute break.

Ways to borrow (1¼ hours)

Purpose
In this part of the meeting, participants will look at available sources of credit. They will also deal with how to tap these sources for their own needs.

Materials
Borrowing story/Use story in box
Information on sources of credit, or a resource person who knows about sources of credit
Note: Here are some useful booklets on credit:
—"Women, Money, and Credit" (Newsletter #15): Available from International Women's Tribune Centre, 777 UN Plaza, New York, New York 10017, free.

Steps
1. Ask the participants what they think credit means. After some ideas are given, explain that credit involves receiving cash or goods now and paying back later, usually with a "rental fee" or interest.
2. Have the women talk about some reasons they may want to use credit. If the group participated in the meetings on "Women and Work," discuss the need for credit for starting small businesses or cooperatives.
3. Read the "Borrowing Story"

"Borrowing Story"

When (Name) returned from visiting her sister in (Town), she was excited to tell her friends what she'd discovered. The friends had wondered how they could be together and earn more money at the same time. During her visit, (Name) found a way!

She told her friends about a small coffee shop she'd seen. It was a place where people relaxed and talked. It was busy all the time. There was nothing like that in their community.

(Name) and her friends talked about starting a coffee shop. They were enthusiastic. They were sure it would be a success..... But—how could they get started?

The friends realized they would need some initial money or capital for renting a place and purchasing supplies. They themselves, and their families didn't have all the money needed.

How could they borrow it? Which way would be best for them?

4. Then, divide the women into groups of four or five members. Tell them to discuss how the woman in the story could get credit if she lived in their community. What are the advantages and disadvantages of the different ways. Take about 20 minutes for the small group discussions.

5. Bring the whole group back together, and ask someone from each group to report on the discussion. As each person reports, write down the suggested ways to get credit. Here are some ways to include on the list:

—Friends and relatives   —Credit associations or cooperatives   —Special government loan programs
—Money-lenders   —Community revolving loan funds   —Foreign aid agencies or embassies
—Shopkeepers   —Banks   —United Nations agencies

6. If you have a resource person at the meeting, bring her/him into the discussion at this point. You or the resource person can help the participants with these questions:
   - What do you know about the ways of credit listed? For the ones no one knows about, where can information be gotten?
   - Has anyone tried a source of credit? What happened?
   - What are the pros and cons of some of the different sources?
   - What seems to be the best source or sources of credit for women in their community?

Ideas to take home
Credit is a very important need for women. Women in your program may only know about borrowing from relatives or money-lenders. At the end of the meeting, help them plan how they will find out more information or what they will do to try to get credit. They may need assistance in making contact with other resource people, or in making visits to banks or credit associations. Your support can really help them get going!

Organizing for community problem-solving

Many women are already making great contributions to the improvement of their communities. Others may be interested but have few opportunities to participate. In the four meetings in this section, women identify priority community problems and plan to take action to solve them.

The meetings take the women through a series of steps for community problem-solving. Meeting 12 helps the women examine why people resist or support change. They also talk about good leadership. In Meeting 13, the women discuss and select priority community problems. Next, in Meeting 14, they identify local resources that can help their problem-solving efforts. They also consider effective ways to approach local officials and authority figures for assistance.

Meeting 15 involves the women in analyzing the causes of certain problems. Then, they prepare plans of action to solve the problems.

As a result of the meetings, women become more involved in their communities. The communities gain a valuable resource for development.

Promoting community improvements

Change in our communities (1½ hours)

Purpose
In this activity, participants discuss reasons why people resist or support ideas for community improvements. In meetings 13, 14, and 15 women will make their own plans for solving community problems. This meeting helps them know how to gain the support of others for their plans.

Materials
"Before" and "After" Community Drawings
   Make your own using samples on page 80-82

Steps

1 Show participants the "Before" community drawing. Discuss with them what they see in the picture: how do people who live there feel? what kind of life do they have? what are the problems they face?

2 Then, show the "After" picture. Ask again the questions in Step #1.

3 Now, tell participants to think about how the community changed from "Before" to "After." Ask them why they think the community changed. How did the changes happen? Point out that the community members must have wanted to improve their community. They probably worked together to do so.

4 Brainstorm (list without discussing) with participants about why community members would support change. Put the ideas on newsprint or a blackboard using either symbols (stick figures) or words. Some of the reasons to include are:
   —they thought the change would benefit them
   —they could afford the change (it wasn't too expensive)
   —they helped make the decision about the change
   —they understood what the change was about
   —they didn't have to risk much to change
   —they had access to necessary resources (such as local "experts," training, and so on)
   —they saw community leaders and friends accept a change
   Add participants' ideas.

5 After participants have identified a number of reasons, hold up the "Before" picture again. Ask participants to pretend that they are living in this community. What would they do to promote improvements? How would they begin?

6 Divide participants into groups of four or five members. Each group will create a skit showing how they would begin to initiate change in their community.

7 Give the groups about 20 minutes to create their skits. Spend time with each group to be sure members understand what to do and what to include in their skit. Tell them to consider:
   —who they will contact (leaders, everyone, one person in every household, and so on)
   —what they will do (hold a meeting, visit house to house, and so on)
   —what they will say.
All members of each group should help plan the skit. But each group can decide the number of members who will act in the skit.

8 Have each group present its skit.

9 After the skits are finished, bring everyone together for discussion:
   • What did each group do in the skit to promote change?
   • How would community members react if you tried this in your own community?

12

• Would community members support the change? Why or why not? (Mention some of the reasons given before about why people might change.)
• What did you find out in the meeting that could be useful in your own community?

Ideas to take home

In the next meetings, the women will work together on solving community problems. Help them to end this activity with some specific ideas that will be useful to them.

Take a short break.

What is a good leader? (about 30 minutes)

Purpose

This activity helps participants think about the qualities of a good community leader. The women may think "leaders" are only people with an official title. Help them to understand that they all can be unofficial leaders. They can encourage their communities to take action to improve.

Materials

Newsprint and felt tip pens (or blackboard and chalk)

Steps

1. Ask participants "What is a leader?" They might talk only about someone with an official title. Point out that everyone in the room can be a leader in promoting community change. We don't need a title to encourage our neighbors to work together.

2. Now ask, "What is a good leader? What qualities and skills does a leader need?" Brainstorm (list without discussing) and record the ideas (see box for examples).

Ideas for Good Leadership

Here are ideas from one group about ways to be a good leader:

1. A good leader finds out what people in the community need. She helps them plan how to get it.
2. A leader speaks out to officials about what is important to people in the community.
3. A leader makes people feel helpful.
4. A leader listens.
5. A good leader gets many different people to work together.

Ideas to take home

Summarize the list and add your own ideas. To end the session, ask participants:

• What do you know now that you didn't know before you came here today?

Materials

12

82

Identifying priority problems 13

Doing a problem survey (1¼ hours)

Purpose
In this meeting, participants identify some community problems. They also decide which of these problems are most important. The "problem survey" activity takes them on a community visit to look for the problems.

Materials
Visit the community, if convenient

Steps

1. Begin by asking the women to think about problems in their community. Ask them to give examples. Now, explain that they will visit their own community to find out some other problems as well. Or, if a visit is not convenient, explain that they will meet in small groups to talk about community problems.

2. Have everyone choose a partner for the community visit. Ask the whole group to give ideas of the kinds of problems to look for. Make a list of the ideas. Literate members can copy the list and take it with them. Here are some things to include on the list:

—Health —Homes —Work
—Transportation —Elderly —Agriculture, food
—Children —Local Organizations —Water, electricity, fuel
—Community Services —Sanitation —Land

If the group does not visit the community, divide members into small groups to discuss the problems. See the box for examples of problems other groups have found.

> ### Some community problems in Northeast Thailand
> Thai women found these problems in their villages:
> —no groups working together for cooperative production and sale of goods
> —no piped water
> —lack of electricity
> —lack of a nearby health center
> —no child care facilities
> —bad roads; lack of public transportation
> —lack of police
> —bad village chief
> —lack of community members having needed technical skills and knowledge
> —villagers who don't cooperate and help one another.

3. Guide the participants in preparing for the community visit. Tell them that two ways to find out problems are: **observing** and **talking to people.** Ask them:
   - Where will you go? (market, schoolyard, fields, along the streets, and so on)
   - Who will you talk to? (leaders, people sitting outside shops, people at home, people at work, and so on)
   - What will you say?

   Encourage them to go to different places and to talk to different people.

4. Ask everyone to return in 45 minutes to 1 hour. If they can take more time, the survey will be more complete. However, in one hour, they can get several ideas about community problems. If the group cannot visit the community, help the small groups discuss community problems.

Ideas to take home
The field can help the women see things in their community. They will return with some very specific stories about community problems.

Selecting priority problems (45 minutes)

Purpose
By the end of this activity, the women will choose community problems they believe are most important. In Meetings 14 and 15, they will plan how to solve these problems.

Materials
One large sheet of newsprint or paper
Tape
5 cm. x 5 cm. (2 in. x 2 in.) (approximately) pieces of colored paper (any colors) to use as ballots
Cassette tape recorder and tape, if available

Steps

1 Bring the group back together. Ask the pairs or small groups to talk about the problems they found. Have each pair or small group report one by one. Ask them:
- What problems did you find?
- Why are they important?

2 If a cassette recorder is available, record the reports.

3 As participants give their reports, write down (with a word or symbol) the problems they say on the large piece of paper. When the reports finish, play back the tape if you made one. Make sure all the problems that participants stated are on the list.

4 Now, point to each problem word or symbol. Have participants say the problem out loud. This helps everyone to remember what the problems are.

5 Give each woman three colored paper squares. Explain that everyone should decide—separately—which three problems she thinks are most important. Then, she can tape one square next to each of those problem words or symbols. Show how to do this.

6 Take 10-15 minutes for taping the squares.

7 When everyone finishes, talk about "priority problems." Explain that we can see a number of problems in our lives. We can't solve all these problems at the same time. But, we can start with problems we think are most urgent. Later, we can solve other problems too. Ask participants to look at the problems listed:
- Which problems have the most colored squares?
- Why were these problems chosen?
- Are these problems the women would like to try to solve? Why? Or, why not?

Ideas to take home
This meeting ends with the women knowing several important community problems. Explain that in the next few meetings, they will choose and plan how to solve one or two problems.

Preparation for Meeting 15

For Meeting 15, you will need to prepare some photographs or drawings.

You will need ten to fifteen pictures. Have at least one picture for each of the problems listed in Meeting 13. The pictures should show some aspect of the problem. However, they don't need to be exact representations of the problems.

The pictures will be used for discussion and analysis. It will be easier for the participants to do this if the pictures are large size—12.5 cm. x 17.5 cm. or 20 cm. x 25 cm. (5 in. x 7 in. or 8 in. x 10 in.) if possible.

If you have a camera and film available, photos are better than drawings. Participants will recognize the scenes from their own communities. If there is time, take the photos with the participants or let the participants take them on their own. This might require some training in using the camera. It's a good way to involve the women more in identifying and thinking about community problems.

If you use drawings, get help from a local artist or person who knows how to draw.

Using local resources   14

Identifying and mobilizing community resources (1 hour)

Purpose
This activity enables participants to find resources in their community to help in solving problems. They will also decide how these resources can be mobilized. In the second part of the meeting, the women will discuss how to approach local officials for assistance.

Materials
The paper listing priority problems from Meeting 13 (have this posted when the participants arrive); A large sheet of paper with a rectangle drawn on it: this rectangle represents a map of the participants' community; Three sets of "markers" (about 20 of each), such as: buttons, stones, large beads, pieces of a stick, matches, and so on.

Steps

1. For this activity, you and the participants need your imaginations. Pretend the rectangle is the community. If you like, draw some landmarks such as river, mountains, or roads. Pretend the markers are resources. During the activity, participants will place the resource markers in the rectangle. It's not important to place the resources exactly where they are actually located. What's important for the participants is identifying the resources that exist.

2. Place the community "map" on a table or the floor. Show the participants the rectangle and tell them to pretend this is their community (city, town, village).

3. Talk briefly about "resources." If your group attended Meetings 3 and 4, remind them that they identified personal and community resources to help them reach their individual goals. Point to the paper listing priority problems posted in the room. Explain that we also need resources to solve community problems.

4. Divide the participants into three teams. Give each group one of the three sets of markers. Explain that each set of markers represents one kind of resource: **environmental** (water, roads, etc.), **institutions or services** (banks, schools, health centers, etc.), and **people** (names of specific people in the community who could be of help).

5. Have the three groups meet separately. Group one should identify **environmental** resources. Group two should identify **institutions or services.** Group three should identify **people.** Spend time with each group to help them think of resources.

6. After 15 minutes, bring the groups back to the "map." Ask each group in turn to place markers in the community to represent the resources they identified. Reassure participants they they don't have to put markers exactly where a resource would really be located in the community. This isn't a geography lesson!

7   When all groups have placed their markers, begin discussion.

8   Discuss the resources that have been identified and how these resources can be mobilized. Some questions to use:
    • Can the group think of any more resources not already on the map: **environmental? institutional/service? people?** (when any is added, put another marker)
    • What resources exist outside the community? (place any markers around the outside of the rectangle)
    • What resources has anyone in the group used? When? Why? What happened?
    • What resources can we use to solve the problems on our list? How?

Ideas to take home

Review all the resources the participants identified on the map. Compliment them on their work. Summarize the ideas they suggested about how to mobilize the resources.

Participants should end this ctivity with a clear idea of what resources exist in their community and how to tap them.

Take a short break.

Communicating with authority figures (1 hour)

Purpose
To solve community problems, the women in your program may need assistance from authority figures: local leaders, government officials, bankers, and so on. Women are often hesitant to communicate with these people, most of whom are men. This activity provides the participants with practice in approaching and making requests of authorities.

Materials
Skit instructions/See instructions on page 88

Steps

1   Explain that the first part of the meeting looked at three kinds of resources: environmental, institutional/service, and people. Ask participants to think about how to approach people who would be useful resources. Has anyone contacted local officials or experts? What happened?

2   Now, prepare the skits. Follow instructions in the box.

3   Ask questions to analyze what happened in the skits. Then, have participants define what to remember to help them in communicating with authority figures. Ask:
    • How did you feel in the skits? Were you comfortable? Uncomfortable?
    • What happened in the skits?
    • What were the problems in communicating with the authorities?
    • Are the problems similar to a real life situation? How?
    • What are some things to remember when we meet with someone in a position of authority? How should we behave?

Ideas to take home
Make sure that participants identify some specific ideas about approaching authority figures. Contribute your own ideas, too. Participants may tend to emphasize that respect and deference should be shown to authorities. You can encourage them also to show their own confidence.

Conclude the session by summarizing some of the ideas suggested about communicating with authorities. Ask participants to think about a future meeting with an official and what they plan to do. Have some participants share their ideas.

"Communicating with authority figures" skit instructions

A skit is a short drama or play. The players themselves create the words and story. To prepare the skits:

- Divide the participants into five groups. Each group will present one of the skits below. If there are less than five groups, have some groups do two skits or use fewer skits.
- Meet with each group. Read the description of the skit.
- Explain that group members will be actors and present a story like actors in a play.
- Ask the group members to create a story for the skit and to name the characters. They should decide what each character will say and do. The group should also decide who will play each character.
- Encourage the group to make the story lively and interesting.
- Give the groups some time to practice the skits.

Have the groups present their skits. Use the questions in Step #3 (p. 87) for discussion.

Skit –1

You and a group of friends are seeking a loan from your local bank. This is your first appointment with a bank official.

Skit –2

Your cousin's children and your own eldest children are ready to start school. You visit the school together to enroll them.

Skit –3

A local health official visits your home to ask about what illnesses your children have had and whether they have been immunized. Your husband is not at home.

Skit –4

Your women's group is concerned because you are losing the local coop, the place you bought things you needed cheaply. A new road is planned. The coop building must be torn down because it is in the way. Your group visits a local government official to discuss the problem.

Skit –5

You want a job at a local factory (or restaurant, farm, or other workplace). This is your meeting with the employer to apply for a job.

Analyzing problems and planning how to solve them 15

Discussing problem pictures
(45 minutes)

Purpose
In this meeting, participants will choose a priority problem and plan how to solve it. The first activity helps participants learn how to identify causes of the problems and to examine alternative solutions. The second activity produces concrete action plans.

Materials
10-15 pictures (photos or drawings) representing problems participants identified in Meeting 13. See "Preparation for Meeting 15" on page 85.

Steps

1. Explain that in this meeting participants will plan how to solve some of the problems they identified in Meeting 13. Divide the group into teams of four to five members each.

2. Tell participants that each team will be talking about one problem and what the members can do about it.

3. Spread all the pictures on a table or the floor. Ask each team to choose one picture which shows a problem that is important to team members.

4. Have each team go to a separate part of the room with its picture. Each team should put the picture where it can be seen by all the members.

5. Now, explain that you'd like the teams to talk about the pictures using a series of questions. Ask one of the questions below at a time. Allow teams a few minutes to talk about it. While they are talking, visit each team and encourage the analysis. Then, follow the same procedure for the rest of the questions.

    NOTE: For literate groups, write the questions on newsprint and post them on the wall. However, make sure to follow the procedure just described for having the teams discuss each question for a set period of time. Otherwise, the teams may discuss the questions too quickly and not thoroughly enough.

Here are the basic questions to ask. You may need to ask other questions to each individual team to stimulate discussion.

- What is this picture about? What do you see happening in it?
- If there are people in the picture, how do you think they feel? How would you feel if you were in the picture?
- Why are things the way they are in the picture? What are the causes of the problem?
- What can we do together to solve this problem? What are some different solutions?
- What seems to be the best way to solve this problem?

Ideas to take home
After the teams have completed their discussions, ask a member from each team to report to the full group. Then, summarize the reports. Restate what each team has decided to do about the problem it chose.

Take a five minute break.

Planning how to solve the problem (1 ¼ hours)

Purpose
This activity will improve the participants' skills in planning how to solve a problem. Participants make a plan of action for solving the problems chosen in the previous activity.

Materials
Poster size drawing of a woman dressed wrong—with clothing that should be under other clothing instead of on the outside/Make your own using the sample on page 91

Sample "Planning Chart"/Make your own using sample on page 92

Large pieces of paper or cardboard, at least 60 cm. x 90 c.m (2 ft. x 3 ft.) (one for each team); colored paper and felt tip pens; scissors; glue (or, charts already prepared)

Steps
1. Show the participants the picture of the woman with her clothes on in the wrong order. Ask participants to tell you what's wrong with the picture. Then, explain the purpose of the meeting. Tell them that their teams will be making plans for solving the problems discussed in the previous activity. What does a plan mean? Basically, it means we have certain things to do. And those things need to be done in some order—some need to be done first, then second, and so on. The woman in the drawing confused the order of the things she had to do!

2. Ask participants if they remember the earlier meeting (Meeting 4) on planning to reach a personal goal. Have them recall what a plan means to them and give examples of a plan. Take a few minutes on this discussion so participants have time to remember some ideas about planning.

3. Ask participants to remember their "Five Friends" for planning: Why? Who? How? When? What? (see page 41).

4. Show the teams the sample planning chart. Explain that each team will make or be given a planning chart. In each pocket, the team will put a "task card" which describes (in symbol or words) a particular task. This is the **How?** of the "Five Friends." In addition, the teams should talk about **Why? Who? When?** and **What?**

    NOTE: Participants used the charts earlier in Meeting 8.

5. Allow the teams about 30-40 minutes to make their planning charts and to create their plans of action.

6. While the teams are making their plans, visit each team and talk with members about what they need to do to solve their problem. Help each team identify some specific tasks.

7. Teams will be proud of their charts. Have each team present its chart and describe their steps (How?) and answer the other "Five Friends" questions: Why? Who? When? What?

Ideas to take home
Ask the teams if the group wants to carry out all the plans or if they want to work together on only one or two. The decision is up to them. End the session when a decision has been reached.

If possible, keep the charts for participants to use again.

Materials 15

Sample planning chart

One of the groups in Thailand decided that an important community problem was that people didn't work together. They decided to start a cooperative small business for producing cloth.

Here is a sketch of the group's planning chart and a list of their problem-solving tasks.

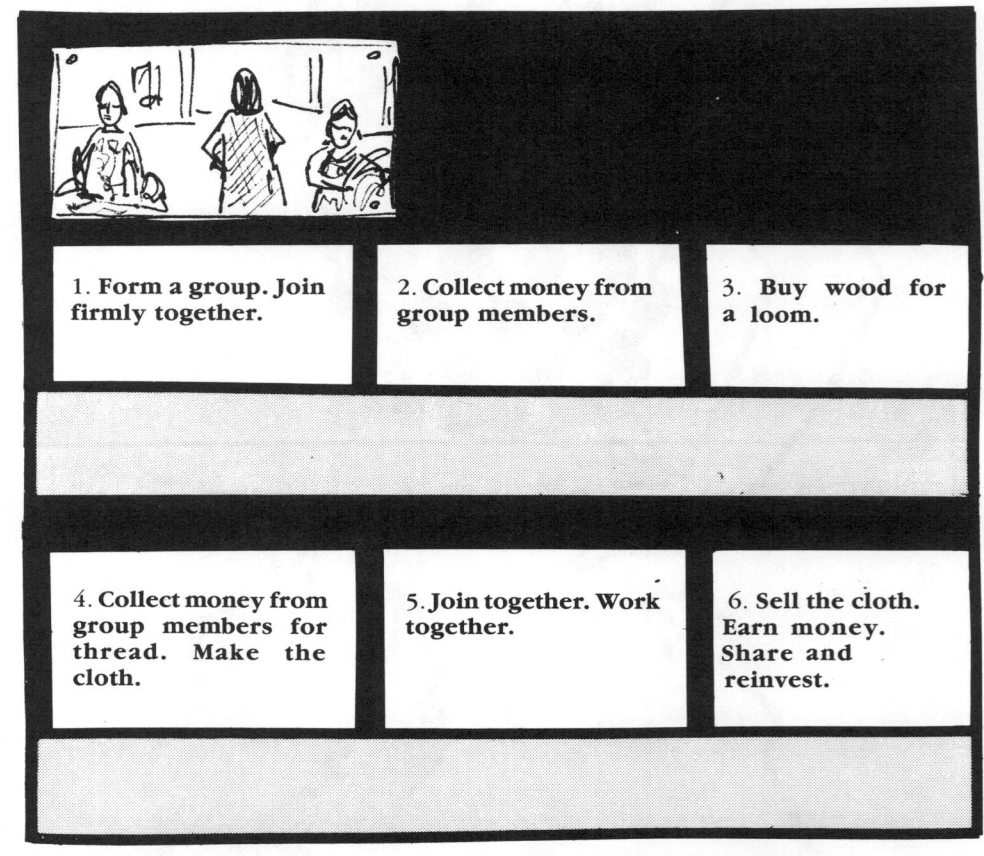

1. Form a group. Join firmly together.

2. Collect money from group members.

3. Buy wood for a loom.

4. Collect money from group members for thread. Make the cloth.

5. Join together. Work together.

6. Sell the cloth. Earn money. Share and reinvest.

The group was successful in producing and selling cloth. In solving the problem, some of the steps in the plan changed. For instance, the group was able to get some used looms at a very low price instead of building them. They also needed to add some other steps.

However, the group's initial plan was what helped them get started. The plan made them feel confident about what they could accomplish together.

Making a Planning Chart

To make a flexible chart you will need a large piece of cardboard or poster board and several heavy strips of paper as wide as the large board. Glue the bottoms and ends of the strips to the board. Folded slips of paper containing "tasks" can then be inserted into the "pocket" made by the strips.

Adapted from: *The Impertinent PERT Chart* by Lyra Srinavasan, (New York: World Education, January 1977).

Women's rights

This section examines women's rights, as individuals and as citizens.

Meeting 16 focuses on the rights of a person in relationships with others. Different kinds of "encounters" are presented for the women to consider. In Meeting 17, the women meet with a resource person familiar with the law. They discuss their rights related to marriage, children, work, voting, taxes, and government services.

These meetings combine skills practice and information-sharing. Women learn more about their rights and how to secure them.

For more information on women and the law, see OEF's *"Empowerment and the Law: Strategies of Third World Women"* (page 104).

Preparation for Meeting 17

For the next meeting, you will need a resource person, such as a lawyer, who knows about the legal rights of women in your setting. It is very important to have a resource person for this meeting. If you cannot find someone to attend, then learn about legal rights yourself before the meeting.

To prepare for the meeting, ask the resource person to review the questionnaire on page 99. The resource person should come to the meeting knowing the answers to these questions.

Personal rights   16

Understanding our personal rights (1-2 hours)

Purpose
This is a skills development meeting. Participants gain more understanding of their rights as individuals and practice behaving in ways that help their rights to be respected.

Materials
"What Would You Do?" questions/Use questionnaire on page 96
Skit instructions/Use instructions on page 97

Steps

1. Start by noting that we all have been in a situation where someone seems unfair to us. Ask participants to give some examples from their own lives.

2. Explain that in these situations, we can react in three ways:
   - We can do nothing (passive)
   - We can get angry and offensive, and make the other person feel that way too (aggressive)
   - We can explain our concerns and try to resolve the situation (assertive)

   Often "assertive" behavior is most helpful where we feel someone has been unfair to us. The ways in which individuals, prticularly women, "stand up for" their individual rights vary among cultures. Discuss the meaning of "assertive" behavior in your participants' setting.

3. Explain to the women that you will read a questionnaire describing some situations. Ask them to choose what they think is the best way to behave in each situation. For literate groups, pass out copies of the questionnaire. Also, if groups are interested ask them to tell which answer is "assertive," "aggressive," and "passive."

4. Read the eight situations on the questionnaire. Help the participants if they have difficulty in deciding which answer would be best. Why did they make each choice? What will the results be?

5. Finish the questionnaire and discussion. Take a short break.

6. Now prepare the skits. Follow instructions on page 97.

7. After each skit, ask participants to give their reactions. What kind of behavior was presented? What was the result? Would other behavior have gotten a better result?

8. Now, help participants consider ways to express their rights in their daily lives. Ask, for example:
   - Think of one situation where you would like to behave in a new way. What would you do? What would the results be?
   - Is it ever good to be passive? to be aggressive? why or why not?
   - What are some effective ways to deal with someone who is unfair to you?

Ideas to take home
Summarize some of the ideas suggested by participants about what they will do in their own lives. At the end of the meeting, participants should have ideas for how to secure their individual rights.

Materials

"What would you do?" questionnaire

Read Situation #1 aloud. Read the three responses to the situation. Ask participants to choose the one response they think is best. Discuss why they think it is best.

Use the same procedure for Situations #2-8.

1. A friend borrowed your largest cooking pot over a week ago. Your relatives are coming for a visit and you need the pot. When you see your friend, you say:
    —I must cook a big dinner on Saturday.
    —How inconsiderate you are to borrow something and not return it.
    —I'll need my pot later this week. Would you return it by Friday?

2. You took your child to the health center for an immunization. You had to wait a long time to see the nurse. When you arrive home, your husband is waiting and wants to know why dinner isn't ready.
    —I'm sorry. I'll prepare it now.
    —There was a long line at the health center. If you watch the children, it won't take me long to cook.
    —How can I do everything? You never understand that.

3. You're buying some fabric to make a new dress. The clerk gives you change for ($5) but you gave her ($10). You point this out and she insists that she was right.
    —You cheat—I'll never come to this store again.
    —Well, I'm not sure I had $10.
    —I'm sure I gave you $10. Would you check again, or tell me where I can find the manager?

4. You make a mistake on your job. Your superior discovers it and tells you harshly that you should not have been so careless.
    —I'll never let it happen again.
    —I did make a mistake and I'll try to be more careful. But please don't be so harsh.
    —It's not my fault. The materials you buy are no good.

5. You and your women's group arrive at the bank for a two o'clock appointment with an officer about a loan. At three o'clock, the officer says that you must wait thirty minutes more to see him.
    —We were here on time and have waited an hour. Would you explain the delay?
    —Yes sir.
    —Other people don't have to wait so long. Why are you so inconsiderate to us?

6. Your son wants to see a movie with his friends. You don't have enough money for the movie and for the new pen he also wants.
    —Well, money is short, but go ahead.
    —You know we don't have much money. You're so selfish.
    —Well, let's talk about it. We're low on money so you have to make choices about what you want.

7. At a community meeting, a woman older than you suggests that you join the community child care committee. You are already on another committee and have a job too.
    —I believe that this committee is very important. But, I can't do a good job on the committee with my other responsibilites.
    —If you really need me, I'll try.
    —No. I'm too busy. You know all the things I have to do.

8. You are at a meeting about community sanitation called by a government health workers. He says the community should start using poison to control rats. You disagree. You raise your hand and he calls on you:
    —I wonder if that's the best thing to do.
    —I'm concerned with having poison around young children. Let's look at the other ways to deal with the problem.
    —I don't like your idea.

16

"Personal rights" skit instructions

A skit is a short drama or play. The players themselves create the words and story. To prepare the skits:
— Divide the participants into four groups. Each group will present one of the skits below. If there are less than four groups, have some groups do two skits or use fewer skits.
— Meet with each group. Read the description of the skit.
— Explain that group members will be actors and present a story like actors in a play.
— Ask the group members to create a story for the skit and to name the characters. They should decide what each character will say and do. The group should also decide who will play each character.
— Give the groups some time to practice the skits.

Have the groups present their skits. Use the questions in steps 7 and 8 for discussion (p. 95).

Skit #1
Your husband has had an argument with another man in your community. The man's wife is a good friend of yours. Your husband tells you he does not want you to visit your friend's house or her to visit your house.

Skit #2
The tax collector tells you that you owe $20. In your training program, you learned about taxes and you know that you really owe #15.

Skit #3
At a community meeting, your community leader asks for four men to volunteer to accompany him to a meeting with a local government official. The community leader says that women do not know how to talk with officials.

Skit #4
Your neighbor borrowed $3 when her child was sick two months ago. You now need the money to buy your daughter some school supplies. But your neighbor has not paid you back.

Legal rights

Knowing our legal rights (2 hours)

Purpose
This meeting will help the participants know their legal rights and what action they can take if their rights are violated.

Materials
"What Are Our Basic Legal Rights?"/Use questions on page 99 Resource person knowledgeable about women's legal rights Available written information on family and work codes

Steps

1 Sometimes resource persons tend to present long lectures. Promote discussion between the resource person and the participants. During the meeting, ask the resource person questions to help him/her focus. Encourage participants to ask questions also.

2 Before the resource person comes into the meeting room, explain to the women that this meeting will deal with women's legal rights. You've invited an expert on the subject.

3 Read the questions on "What Are Our Basic Legal Rights?" Ask participants to give their answers and record them. Stress that this is not a test. It's a chance for them to compare their ideas with information the expert provides.

4 Now, introduce your resource person. Read the questions on "What Are Our Basic Legal Rights?" again. Have the resource person answer each question.

5 Discuss the answers to the legal rights questions. Encourage the resource person to add any additional information. Encourage the participants to ask further questions.

6 When the questions have been answered, discuss what to do when one's rights are violated. Ask these questions to the resource person and participants:
   - Can you think of a situation when your rights or the rights of a friend/relative were violated? What happened? What did you/they do?
   - What can we do when our rights are violated (give specific examples related to work, children, marriage, and civil rights)?

Ideas to take home
To end the meeting, ask participants to state any new information they got from the meeting. Participants may not remember all the laws, but this can help them remember those which are most important.

17

What are our basic legal rights?

1. At what age does a woman reach legal majority (gain legal rights)? What rights does she gain?

2. At what age can a woman marry? What are other laws about marriage?

3. Under what circumstances can a husband divorce his wife? a wife her husband?

4. If a couple divorces, how is it decided whether the mother or father takes custody of the children?

5. Can a married woman own her own property? Can a single or divorced woman?

6. If a woman's father and/or mother dies, who inherits the possessions and property?

7. If a woman earns wages:
    a. does the employer have to pay a minimum daily or hourly salary? If so, how much?
    b. how many hours a week should the woman work? when is she entitled to overtime?
    c. what benefits must be provided by the employer?
    d. does she get paid maternity leave? how long? who pays?
    e. can she be fired if she gets pregnant?

8. What are the laws pertaining to voting for local and national officials? What does a person have to do to be eligible to vote? Does she have to register? How?

9. Who determines how much you must pay in taxes? How do they determine this?

10. Up to what age is it obligatory for a woman to attend school? for a man?

11. What services is the government required to provide to you (education, health, child care, public works, and so on)? How can you obtain these services?

12. Does a married woman have the right to spend the money she earns or inherits?

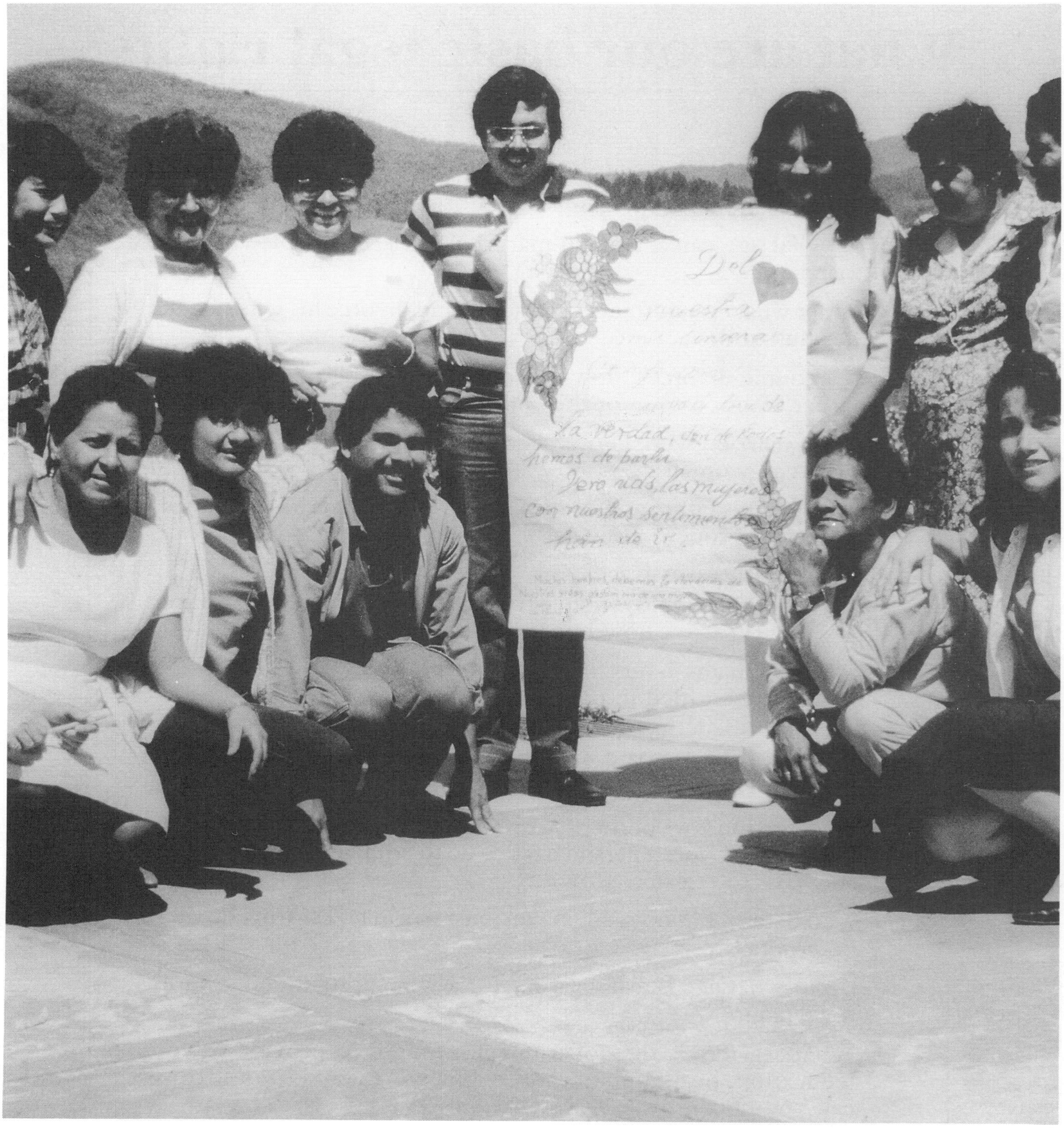

From learning group to action group

The final meeting in the program guides the women in looking back and in looking ahead.

The first part of the meeting gives the women a chance to appreciate what they've accomplished. The second part involves them in discussing "what's next?"

The meetings in your program brought women together. The women developed new awarenesses and skills. They initiated personal, economic, and community development activities. The women have been prepared for self-reliance. They are ready to move from learning group to action group!

What have we accomplished? Where do we go from here?

Looking back (about 1 hour)

Purpose
During the program, the women in your group have gotten to know each other and to work together. Now is the time for them to decide if they want to continue to meet together. If they do want to continue, what do they want to do? To help them decide, in the first part of the meeting, they think about what they accomplished in the program. In the second part, they discuss ideas for continuing activities.

Materials
Goal name tags (from Meeting 3), and Problem-solving charts (from Meeting 15), if available

Materials for making collages: paper, cardboard, magazines, felt tip pens, glue, scissors (a collage is a picture made from a variety of materials)

Steps

1. Start the meeting by telling participants some of your own feelings and thoughts about the program. You might talk about: any changes you saw in the group, what you think the members accomplished, and some special happy memories.

2. Now, encourage the women to share their own thoughts about the program. If you have the goal name tags from Meeting 3, pass them out. If you have the charts from Meeting 15, put them up. Ask them to think about what they have gained and accomplished. Have a few participants answer these questions:
   - How have your **feelings about yourselves changed?**
   - What **personal goals** have been achieved?
   - What **income generation plans** have been pursued?
   - What **community problem-solving** activities are underway or planned?
   - Have **relationships with family and community members** changed? How?

   Take about 15 minutes for this discussion. The women will have more time to talk about their thoughts later.

3. Ask each participant to think about the most valuable thing she got from the program. Explain that everyone will make a collage to describe her ideas. A collage is a picture that you make with many things: drawings, cut-out pictures from magazines, pieces of paper or cloth, and so on.

4. Have the participants work on their collages. This will take about 20 minutes.

5. Bring the group back together. Ask everyone, in turn, to show her collage and explain what it means.

Ideas to take home
Compliment the group, again, on what they accomplished during the program. Help group members end this activity feeling an appreciation for themselves and one another.

Take a five minute break.

18

Looking ahead (about 1 hour)

Purpose
The program gave the participants a series of meetings to attend. In this final activity, participants make their own plans for continuing meetings.

Materials
Paper or newsprint and felt tip pens may be needed

Steps

1. Remind the women that this is the last planned meeting in the program. It is now up to them to plan their own activities. What would they like to do?

2. Divide participants into groups of four or five members. Have each small group talk about ideas for continuing group activities. Give them some examples from other groups to guide them (see box).

Ideas for continuing activities
Here are some activities women in other countries planned and carried out:
- starting a chicken-raising cooperative
- securing rights to agricultural land
- beginning a community child care center
- getting a bank or credit coop loan to start a small business
- finding new marketing channels for crops and other products.

3. Take about 20 minutes for the small group discussions. During the discussion, visit each group and give them suggestions for things to think about if necessary.

4. Ask everyone to get back together. Have each small group give the ideas from their discussions.

5. Now, ask the group to discuss:
   - Which ideas for continuing activity are of most interest?
   - What are the pros and cons of the different ideas?
   - What activities would the group like to do? What needs to be done and who will do it? When?

Guide the group in making the decisions.

Ideas to take home
Before this meeting ends, encourage the group to define WHAT they want to do, WHEN they want to do it, and WHO will do it. Also, explain what your own plans are and whether you can continue to meet with the group. Ask the group to decide when and where the next meeting will be.

Have the participants been planning a final party? End the meeting with some discussion of the celebration!

Other Training Resources

Business Skills for Women Entrepreneurs

This series, of training manuals originally developed and produced by the Overseas Education Fund (OEF) explores how to consider non-traditional work options, how to develop marketable skills, how to access credit, and how to manage and market a business. For use by experienced trainers, programmers, and extension agents, the training activities presented in these two manuals enable either urban or rural women with little or no literacy or numeracy skills to start or make a small enterprise more profitable.

Marketing Strategy: Training Activities for Entrepreneurs, 96 pages plus gameboard. ISBN# 0912917-08-3 US$15.50. Also available in Spanish and French.

This handbook features an innovative board game- "Marketing Mix"- proven especially effective with illiterate groups as well as literate ones. Designed for women with existing businesses, the game introduces the four key aspects of marketing: product, distribution, promotion and price. After playing "Marketing Mix", participants examine marketing methods in their own businesses and identify concrete ways to improve their practices and increase sales.

Doing a Feasibility Study: Training Activities for Starting or Reviewing a Small Business, Suzanne Kindervatter, ed., and others, 176 pp, ISBN# 0-91297-07-5 US$17.00

Women who want to start or change a business explore a range of enterprise options and develop a business plan and a budget. Participants learn how to "research" the viability of an enterprise themselves, investigating market demand, costs, and income projections. By actually conducting a "feasibility study", women gain important skills in problem-solving and management.

Gender Analysis for Grassroots Workers

Another Point of View: A Gender Analysis Training Manual for Grassroots Workers, by Rani Parker, 106 pp., UNIFEM, US$15.95

Another Point of View is a transformative tool which recognizes people's ability to assess their own lives and chart a course of action for change. It uses as a primary tool the Gender Analysis Matrix, a community-based technique for the identification and analysis of gender differences. The matrix is based on the principle that all required knowledge for gender analysis exists among the people whose lives are the subject of the analysis; outside technical expertise is not required.

This clearly written well designed manual offers a step-by-step guide for conducting a four-day workshop with grass-roots people. It includes a pre-workshop questionnaire, case studies, participant handouts, a workshop evaluation questionnaire, suggestions for workshop follow-up activities, a glossary of terms and a resource section for additional reading.

*   All prices are subject to change
** All orders must be prepaid in US dollars. Please make checks payable to WOMEN, INK. Please add 20% for postage and mail to:

WOMEN, INK.
777 United Nations Plaza, Third Floor,
New York, N.Y. 10017, USA
Tel: (212) 687 - 8633 Fax: (212) 661 - 2704